Outside the Frame:
A Mother's Journey Through Autism

Ellie Duley

Copyright © 2021 by Ellie Duley

All rights reserved. No part of this publication may be reproduced, distributed, or transmitted in any form or by any means, including photocopying, recording, or other electronic or mechanical methods, without the prior written permission of the publisher, except in the case of brief quotations embodied in critical reviews and certain other noncommercial uses permitted by copyright law.

Book Design by Prominence Publishing
ISBN: 978-1-988925-87-5

CONTENTS

Part 1: The Early Years   5
Part 2: The Early School Years   50
Part 3: The Aughts   78
Part 4: After the Move   137

INTRO

When I was in college, I thought my life was *so* ordinary. I grew up in the suburbs in Western Massachusetts; two parents, two siblings, a dog, and a few cats, braces, tennis lessons-blah, blah, blah. My junior year in college, I had to write my obituary for one of my journalism classes. I thought this a rather gruesome task. I also had nothing much to say. I wrote about taking two vacations each year-basically, my love of mountains and the ocean. I threw in a broken leg from age 10 when I lost the battle of the mogul field while in a ski lesson in Canada. It was a very short and privileged obit, to be sure!

Many years later I had Jon.

PART 1
THE EARLY YEARS

Raising Jon was hard.

And exhausting.

It was hard physically because he was, and still is, strong. It was hard mentally because he was, and still is, non-verbal and I felt like I was his voice.

It was exhausting because Jon wasn't a great sleeper after his first year, (though I hear that he's doing better in his group home, where he is very happy, probably because he has different rules). It was also exhausting because a lot of worry goes into raising any child and this particular child seemed to be constantly testing me.

This is an account of raising Jon. Done without the journals that I did not keep in the early nineties and through the aughts, and with only the aid of the photos that chronicled the lives of both my boys. Speaking of photos, I recently ran across one that I don't remember being taken. One of very few that I'm in, as I was, apparently, the family historian. It was of me sitting on a couch and holding 15-month-old Jon. He was sleeping in my arms; his light denim shirt pulled away from his darker denim jeans revealing a small bit of his tiny back. My nails were worn too long and perfectly manicured and I was looking directly into the camera while Jon's head was resting near my shoulder. My dark eyes shined and my round, tanned face was peaceful. I was smiling. My dark hair fell loosely down by Jon's small head. His short hair was just slightly lighter than mine, lightened a bit at the temples by the sun. Such a peaceful moment that I don't even remember. When I saw this picture, as I was downsizing from a large house to a much smaller apartment, I cried. Proof that things were calm and peaceful at least for a moment or two of this time raising Jon.

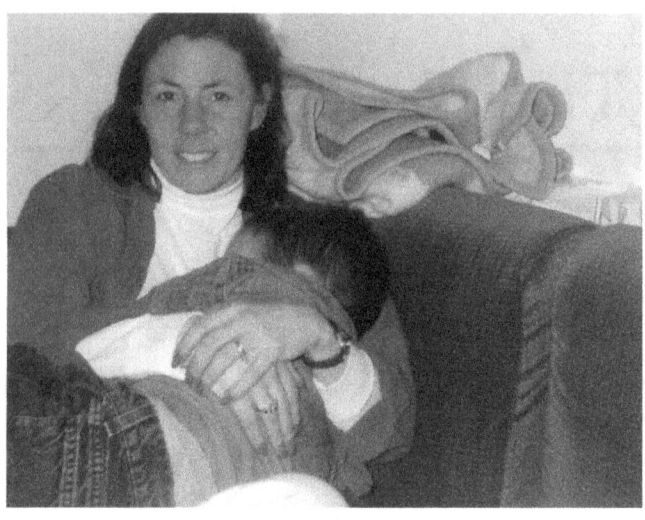

~ ❖ ~

I have two boys. Well, they are men now. The oldest, Bobby, was born in 1989 when I was 27. The younger, Jon, was born in 1991 when I was 28. I had them 16 months apart and my reasoning was quite intentional. I thought that even if they hated each other most of the time, they would, at least, be able to keep each other company on family vacations, (apparently, I planned to keep the vacation theme from my youth alive with my new little family). Being the oldest of three, and the oldest by ten years to my sister, I wanted to do things differently than my parents had.

By the very laws of nature, my plan backfired.

~ ❖ ~

My parents moved from Longmeadow, Massachusetts. To Richmond Virginia the month after I graduated from high school. Just one month after that, I took off for the University of Maine at

Orono. During the summers I worked in the arcade at Kings Dominion. I hate video games and always have-it was far from perfect!

In 1984, I married my college sweetheart in Virginia. Three weeks after graduation. Right? We stayed in Maine and pursued our careers. Dave worked as a management trainee for a Maine grocery chain. Many promotions and a few buyouts later, he is still with that company. I worked as a shoe buyer for a Maine shoe chain. I was responsible for buying all the childrens' shoes for the seven stores in the chain. What woman wouldn't be happy spending someone else's money on shoes? Even if they were for the tiniest of feet. I still have no idea what this had to do with my expected journalism/advertising career, but it was a job that I really loved.

After four years it became almost painfully obvious to us that it was the very best time to start a family. Is there ever a very best time? In any case, with my-at-the-time-type A personality, I was very irritated, when after six months off the pill and four months of trying, I had yet to conceive. My solution was to go to Sugarloaf Mountain in western Maine and have a full-on blowout weekend of spring skiing (I fell at least once) and Après ski drinks. I found out that I was pregnant two days after my return to work.

Bobby is fine.

Pregnancy was uneventful. I pretty much hated it, but it was fine. I worked throughout the pregnancy, even traveling to New York City at seven months along. I had no trouble catching a cab that trip. I just stuck my pregnant belly, clad in ruffled and tent-like maternity dresses that did not suit my frame, into view until a yellow cab pulled over to assist.

A couple of months later, I went in to work the morning that Bobby was born at 4:13 PM. I was five days past my due date. As a Virgo, this was unacceptable. One of my office mates had already called the hospital, (again), to see if I'd been admitted. She didn't want to bother me by calling the landline at home and I was a few minutes late for work that day. I had promised to report any news but perhaps I wasn't coming off as trustworthy during those long five days!

I left the office around noon and went a mile home to get something to eat and rest. I wasn't feeling great. Obviously, I didn't think that I was in labor because it had been burned into my brain to eat lightly before having the baby.

My abdomen felt strange, but I had been assured that I would magically know when it was time to go to the hospital. I was told that this would feel like menstrual cramps. I wasn't too experienced with cramps, so I made a bagel and liberally spread the cream cheese.

After my lame lunch, I called the doctor and spoke with his wife who listened to my symptoms and instructed me to get my 'in labor' body to the hospital and she would get my doctor and her husband to wait for me. Since it was so close (about a mile) and since I would, literally, speed to my own funeral, I was checked in and examined by 2 PM.

Dave worked an hour away and by the time he arrived I was too dilated to receive any drugs for pain, which I was actually sort of happy about in a strange way. When I called from the hospital after being admitted I told him where my car was parked so that he could grab my Lamaze bag before coming in to see me and the birth of our first child. That was a waste of his time as that baby was ready to be birthed. That kit so carefully and thoughtfully put together, (tennis balls for back massages included), was never opened or thought of again until it was disassembled when we moved 18 months later.

The dog loved those tennis balls.

The day that Bobby was born was a national smoke-out day. I don't know if this is still a thing, but in 1989 smokers could pledge to quit for one day, often in exchange for Tootsie Rolls. I know this because when I was in high school in Massachusetts and a member of the Keyettes, a service club, I would stand outside the grocery store with Tootsie Rolls and ask strangers to sign a pledge to quit for one specific day in November.

No one can say I didn't get my community service hours in!

My labor nurse was one of those people, but years later and in another state. She was at the end of a double shift, so she wasn't super supportive to me at the time of Bobby's birth. Good for her for trying to quit. She did promise me that I would be done with labor by the end of General Hospital. Since he was born 13 minutes after my soap ended, I wanted those thirteen minutes back for years. I'm over it now.

Bobby was the perfect Gerber baby. High forehead, blonde hair, and blue eyes with creamy beautiful skin. I loved him immediately.

I also knocked a full bottle of perfume off my bedside table that first night in the hospital. Why wouldn't I spritz Giorgio immediately after birthing a child? Priorities of a non-mom and a new mom collided within hours of giving birth. I couldn't sleep with that smell and the adrenaline of giving birth.

I haven't worn Giorgio since.

While in the hospital I developed a rash on the palms of my hands and the soles of my feet. It drove me nuts. I couldn't sleep and ended up in the ER a week later on Thanksgiving Day to get some relief. One week in and I wasn't loving motherhood. I loved Bobby, but there was so much else that was going on. My body was a hormone-filled, sleep-deprived mess. I ran hot like a furnace. I was so uncomfortable in so many ways.

After six weeks of the maternity leave that I fought so very hard to get, (I was the first person in the company to get paid maternity leave), I went back to work in early January 1990. I was just starting to feel like myself again and Bobby was just starting to cry less often and for shorter periods of time. He wasn't colicky, but babies cry. A lot. I had a baby book with a diagram of cry cycles corresponding with age. He was pretty spot on with that diagram, which magically lined up with the six-week mark for shorter and fewer crying episodes. I was just getting the hang of this mom thing and it was time to go back to work. He also spit up. A lot. It was hard to find time for a shower. It was definitely not glamorous. I wanted to tell my birth story to anyone who would listen.

It was hard for me to keep up with myself.

But go back to work I did.

I had a week-long buying trip to NYC planned for February, and I was quite sure that I could do it all. Be the perfect mom and wife and be the glue that held the office together. I must have had that power because I took work phone calls almost every single day during the maternity leave (that I fought so very hard to get), in my purple sweatpants that were stretched out from the pregnancy. The ones that Dave hated. Looking back, I was just too tied to my working identity. My 'mom' identity wasn't fully formed yet. I canceled my trip to NYC and went part-time to have more time with Bobby.

Part-time wasn't as satisfying professionally. I was always the last to know things. They say knowledge is power, right? I really wanted to be home with Bobby and hated leaving him at daycare, so I left my job and we started trying for a second baby. For the vacation reason as formerly stated, and for the reason that I wanted two kids, and I wanted to get the second pregnancy over with. The bloating, headaches, and queasiness. All of it.

I was pregnant within a month.

Jon was born on April 3rd. His due date was April 4th so that worked for my personality and astrology sign. I woke at around

2 AM with what I thought were contractions. I had already had a child so I should have known, but I had also spent the previous Friday night/early Saturday morning having Braxton Hicks (fake contractions) at the hospital, while Dave counted the cop cars at the drive-thru at the Dunkin' across the street-you can't make this up.

Anyway, on the early morning of April 3, I was preparing to leave for the hospital while Dave was making coffee and my mother-in-law was preparing for Grammie duty for Bobby during the big event of Jon's eventual birth. It was during the coffee-making that my water broke. I had to change from the ugly purple sweatpants to the permanently stained and stretched-out white ones.

I assume the coffee maker finished making coffee after we left for the hospital. The contractions came hard and fast, and I had to hold onto the wall during these contractions as I slowly walked to the room where Jon was born. It wasn't lost on me that during my dry run with Braxton Hicks I was offered a wheelchair (that I didn't need).

Jon was born just after 3 AM and after about five painful pushes. He was cold and his Apgar wasn't perfect like his brothers, but it was a decent 7-8. He was immediately put into an incubator to warm up. It was suspected, though never confirmed, that his quick entry into the world was responsible for his chills. When I could see him, I remember that I was concerned that one of his ears was pointed. Like Spock. I even asked a doctor about this. Little did I know that this would be the least of my issues/problems/concerns.

Twelve long and uncomfortable and very hungry hours later I had a tubal ligation. I was shutting down the baby factory for good. This was way before I would find out how much of my time would be devoted to Jon's care.

Both boys were born at an inland hospital and when Jon was six weeks old, we moved to the coast. Apparently, I like to do things the hard way.

No stress, there.

Jon was born with dark hair-lots of it-and olive skin. His eyes were a grey that you don't usually associate with newborns. He was beautiful and I loved him deeply. Bobby's looks resembled his father's side of the family and Jon was the swarthy Portuguese twin of an uncle on my mom's side.

Complete gene pool split.

From the moment I held him I felt a special connection that I hadn't felt before. It was like we were of one mind. I felt like I knew when he would cry before he even started crying. I could prepare for it. Warm a bottle or change a diaper. At first, I attributed this to being a second-time mom, but it wasn't long before I knew that this special bond was something beyond description and essential to Jon's development and my sanity. We would communicate through our eyes. This was before he lost all eye contact, (later, and after lots of hard work, he would gain his eye contact back, but I digress).

It was like I knew how he ticked. It was so different from my first experience where I felt clueless all the time. I described this feeling to people, other moms, and they just looked at me with blank eyes. It was after a few of these conversations that I realized that it was a true and special bond.

I stopped trying to define it.

When Jon was very young, he was very strong. He could pull himself up and cruise along the furniture as young as six months old. He didn't trust himself to take that first step until 13 months, but the balance was there.

With time comes trust.

When I took him to his six-month checkup at his doctor's office that was almost across the street, I learned about his furniture walking. The location of his doctor would be important later when I could call to see if they were running on time and had the luxury of being two minutes away. This allowed us to wait at home instead of in the waiting room, but this day we were in the waiting room. He was restless, as six-month-old's can be, so I let him crawl around a bit. He examined some toys and rejected playing with them, so he headed back to me. He pulled himself up on one of the waiting room chairs and headed toward a pair of khaki pants and boat shoes. These were directly in his sightline. He was very surprised, as was the lady dressed like me when he grabbed her knee and looked up to see a stranger's face. I watched the whole thing wanting to see what would happen. It ended up that I just took him back to my chair.

The doctor was very impressed with his gross motor skills.

For the first 18 months, Jon slept for up to 18 hours a day. He was a champion sleeper in the beginning. Sleeping through the night early and keeping the two-a-day nap schedule that all moms want. Looking back and knowing what I know now, I would have tried to engage him more in the world in that first, critical year.

Hindsight is not helpful in this case.

Jon often spent his mere six wakeful hours during those first 18 months smiling and laughing; his eyes gleaming and engaged with the world.

Our little family motored along for the first few years. At times, blissfully unaware.

Since Jon was an infant, and up until puberty, his main goal in life had been to get away from me-the keeper of his freedom. Some people refer to people who exhibit this behavior as bolters.

Jon was a bolter.

This isn't about his bolting, per se, it's more about his ability to escape any torture device in which I placed him. He never did master the escape of the five-point car seat, but the highchair and grocery store cart were the stuff that parental nightmares are made.

The highchair shenanigans started early. I'd say before his first birthday. The first time it happened was a total surprise. He was belted in, like all active toddlers are, one minute, and standing on the seat the next. He wasn't even walking yet, but his desire to leave the table was stronger than any fear of falling that he probably never had.

I think that I must have assumed that the belt wasn't tight enough that first time. He hadn't unbuckled the belt, so it wasn't like he had cracked that code. I began progressively tightening that belt more and more to the point where I was afraid that he wouldn't be able to breathe. He would somehow move and manipulate his body to a standing position without unbuckling anything. I never really saw him do this completely because if I saw him start then I would ask him to stop and tighten the belt.

The reason that I just didn't let him roam free was because he was the fastest eater in the house and would often be done before I even had a chance to sit down to eat. Jon was not a good candidate to roam freely around to house. There was just too much trouble to be had, toilets to play in kitchen cabinets to unload.

It's all about balance.

The grocery store was even worse. This special talent of his was now on public display and the danger level of falling much greater. People saw me crank down the safety belt as tightly as it would go. They might also have seen me turn my back, and look in horror, as I turned back around to see Jon proudly standing in the seat part of the cart. There were signs around the store warning about this activity. The floors were a very solid cement under the shiny linoleum. A young toddler's head was no match for that. To this day, I can't stand to see kids standing in carts even though he never fell.

I don't know if he loosened that belt or just squirmed his body away from it. I also don't know how he got his legs out of the leg openings in the seat. The very leg openings that were so very hard to insert the very same legs into when we first entered the store.

I really don't know how any of it worked. It was his special, and very dangerous, skill.

Bolting wasn't always about getting away from me or a situation. There were times when it was very much about getting to something. That something was almost always water. Lakes, puddles, the dog's water bowl, and toilets to name a few.

They were all in play.

When Jon was just a few weeks old we moved to an ocean community. We spent every sunny summer day at the beach. At first, he napped in his back carrier under an umbrella, but as soon as he learned to walk his devilry began.

The other moms would set up chairs to watch their young kids play in the sand and chase seagulls. Bobby happily joined them in these noble pursuits, whereas Jon needed to be in the water. While my friends were happily sorting out disagreements about which buckets and other sand toys belonged to whom, I was ankle-deep in the frigid Atlantic holding Jon's hand so that he didn't keep walking. I can only assume that his plan was to head to Europe.

I tried to join my friends for some adult conversation, but Jon never saw that particular want or need of mine to be very important.

The first time he did it, I almost didn't catch him. What his plan was, and I have to admit that it was clever, was to scoot or crab walk backward toward the sea. He was very patient and could take several minutes to move just a few feet. When he was at a distance that he deemed far enough from me and close enough to the water, he would hop up, turn quickly, and head across the rocky sand and right into the water. He didn't want to wade into the water like other kids-he was determined to keep walking and I assume, at some point, when the water was over his head, he would just swim away. The first time I ran to get him, we were both a little surprised. He because his plan failed and, I because I caught him. He tried it a few more times before I gave up and went into the water with him. I didn't even bother to bring a chair after a while. I was never able to sit it so why carry it?

~ ❖ ~

Safety was most definitely a concern during the bolting years. Back when I had my first dog, I filled out a form that I got either from the vet or from the reams of direct marketing that was stuffed into the Sunday paper and was a thing back in the '80s. This form was mailed away with a check and eventually produced a small tag for Joe's (the dog) collar which informed anyone who might find him where his owner (I) could be found. I only needed this once when he roamed from the house, probably stopping at his favorite pond at Bates college, and eventually ending up in some woman's apartment. She was lovely enough to call the landline-the only option at the time-to report that she had Joe and that he liked bologna. He was a lab. They eat anything.

It was ten years later that I found myself looking for one of those forms, checkbook in hand when I learned that I could just go to Wal-Mart, type my info in and a tag would be printed. Right away. This new info excited the problem solver in me. I made several tags with Jon's name, address, and our phone number. Those tags were threaded onto the bottom lace of a sneaker and attached to various backpacks and ski jackets. Luckily, I never did get a call that someone was feeding bologna or anything else to my missing child. His bolting almost never worked well enough to get very far away from me.

Jon didn't play with toys like other toddlers. He also didn't play with other kids like other kids, but this is about toys.

As the mom of two young boys, I was very, very, very familiar with LEGOs. Those hard, plastic building toys could entertain for hours. They could also reduce a grown woman to tears and lots of swearing if one was accidentally left in the path of a bare foot.

Between the two boys, I had what seemed like tons of these torture devices on hand. Bobby liked to build things and Jon would sometimes sort them by color or shape. Both were responsible for putting them away at the end of the day.

One of Jon's favorite activities regarding his LEGOs was dumping them out of the big yellow container and walking through a pile of them, scattering them around the room. This explained how some of the smaller ones ended up in the vacuum cleaner-just like Barbie's shoes back in my day. I didn't encourage this behavior because I knew, firsthand, how much it could hurt if a foot landed directly on a LEGO, but he would still just shuffle with bare feet right through the huge pile on the floor. This, by the way, drove his brother crazy.

In any case, there were lots of LEGOs in my life during the years before pre-school. This was 1993 and Jon was two.

During this time, it was obvious that Jon enjoyed jigsaw puzzles as well. At least I thought he did. I had lots of fun putting them together with him. I used the picture on the box to guide me and Jon chose his pieces by their shape, alone. This was all good we had plenty of both LEGOs and puzzles to go around.

At some point, I realized that we really didn't have plenty to go around anymore. Puzzles would be finished with several holes and not enough pieces. I did find some puzzle pieces in the bathroom in a white wicker urn that was stuffed with decorative fake eucalyptus. You may have two questions here: Why fake eucalyptus? No clue? What was I doing to find said pieces? Again, no clue, but find them, I did. Even fake eucalyptus needs occasional dusting, and this was my best guess about what I was doing to find these pieces. Perhaps, Jon wasn't always as sneaky as he and I both thought he was.

This got me thinking. If puzzle pieces were stashed in a wicker urn full of fake greenery, where else might they be stashed?

I had a circa 1970's stereo that had traveled with me to college, a couple of apartments, and two houses. It resided in the living room, complete with two large floor speakers. It's hard to believe I toted all that around when I now use a very small Bluetooth device with my iPhone. Some things were certainly more complicated back then.

In any case, there were cats in the house at that time. One of them, (I'm not really sure which but, probably the huge grey Maine Coon cat named Smokey. You know, because she was grey. Clever), seemed particularly fond of swiping her claws on the back of one of the speakers, which, again, were large and sat on the floor. She did this in the back where I couldn't see the damage-until that day that I did.

One day I went to move the speaker for some unrecallable reason-probably to vacuum; a task that I could only do on Saturday mornings when Dave took the boys to the transfer station to dump a weeks' worth of trash. The sound of the old Electrolux tank that was once my grandmother's would send Jon into orbit. He. Just. Could. Not. Deal. With. That. Sound. This was when I saw that the fabric in the back was falling away from the speaker. As I lifted the speaker to examine the situation, I heard a strange noise inside of it. I decided that a full investigation was in order.

What I found was that one of my imps, undoubtedly, Jon, was peeling back that fabric and inserting objects into the speaker through a hole in the pressboard that, evidently, must have been there to make music sound splendid. That, or I was dealing with a cheap speaker that was 20 years old. Discovering this was one thing but getting the stuff out was entirely another matter.

I hunted down a screwdriver and got to work. After getting the fabric off the speaker and getting the cheap pressboard/plywood removed from the back, I was rewarded with the discovery of Jon's favorite toy dumping ground. This was confirmed by Bobby later. There were over 100 LEGOs and various puzzle pieces in there. He was young, and his antics were still celebrated and considered adorable. Somewhere, I have a picture of that old speaker and the bounty that I retrieved that day.

Back in the early '90's, most family pictures taken by amateur photographers (parents) were done on film. This film needed to be loaded into the camera and later unloaded and taken to a place for developing. I took a lot of photos during the kid's early years and because CVS offered free doubles, I always came home with 48 pictures of mostly the same thing. I still do this, but on my iPhone and with the ability to delete all images except the best ones of my big, black Newfoundland dog. The kids are grown, and habits are hard to change, but technology has been a blessing and I no longer fill up shoeboxes with duplicate pics of basically the same image.

Looking back, there is something funny about all the pics that this family historian took. Jon is either asleep, (one of his two speeds at that time), half out of the frame, lying down (perhaps on his way to sleeping) or someone had what looks like a death grip on him. There is one picture where he had both feet on the floor, clad in tiny blue Keds canvas sneakers, his torso, which has always been long for his short stature, was bent at the waist and lying across a couch cushion. One small hand tucked, ever so slightly, into the waistband of his red courduroys. Another sleeping picture shows Jon sleeping on his back on a pile of sleeping bags with various Disney characters on them. He loved those unzipped and faded bags and would carry them around until he found a suitable corner (in the dining room?) and get them arranged just right until he fell softly to sleep-again with the tips of his fingers tucked into his waistband.

Such a normal guy thing.

There were also pics of his head down in his dinner on the tray of his highchair.

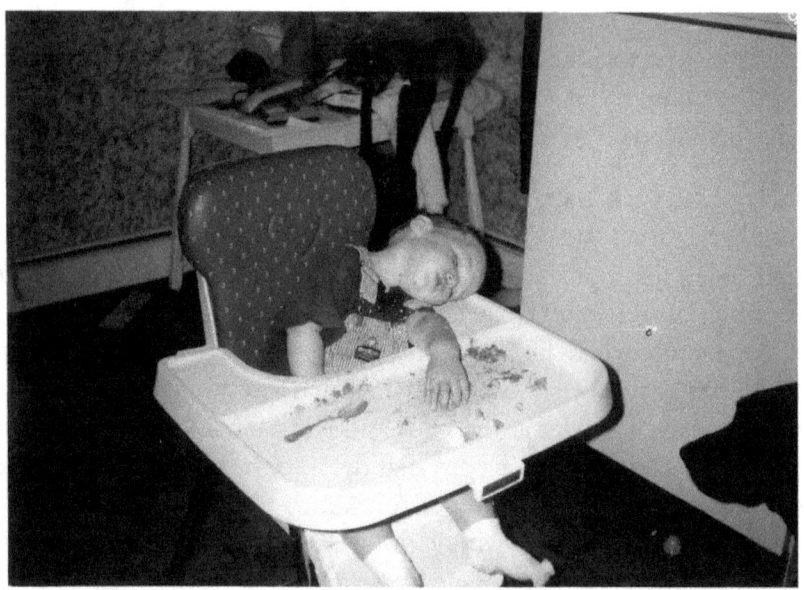

This one happened a lot! Jon once fell asleep while walking. He woke himself up and didn't fall and I wouldn't believe it if I hadn't seen it. His balance has always been amazing. Sadly, there is no photographic evidence of this.

Bobby was the one most often charged with keeping his brother in the picture. Often, with his arm around Jon's neck, (not shoulder, but neck). Whether it was a potential Christmas card picture or a beach snap, Bobby was almost always connected to Jon in some way. I'm not sure if Jon didn't understand what I was attempting to do with the camera or if he actually did and was just being a pain in the neck, but group photos were extremely difficult.

I do have some nice ones of him by himself when he was really small, but he must have tired of the photo thing as he aged. He had a perfect smile with straight tiny white baby teeth and shining eyes that had changed from grey to a beautiful amber and that were as clear as a sunny day.

Back then, his dark hair would lighten from running around the beach every day all summer. Crescent Beach state park was under two miles away from the house so we would spend our mornings there and just pop home for any necessities like lunch, diaper changes, and naps. Now that hair is jet black and thinning-he got the receding (Portuguese) gene. Now, I see a few stray greys in the goatee (that he manages to pull off), which grows so thick and fast. His round face is mostly serious these days, but occasionally he will erupt into giggles that make sense only to him. He was extremely giggly at his brother's recent wedding.

His lack of verbal ability keeps his secret.

Perhaps his seriousness had to do with his feeling uncomfortable though we have no medical knowledge of this. Jon, who has been gluten-free for 20 years, and sees major positive changes in behaviors, was once a gluten glutton. In fact, gluten, a protein found in many popular grains, was the bedrock of his diet for all of his early years.

We went out to restaurants (rarely) when Jon was in his tantrumming stage (18 months to 3 years) and I always immediately asked our server for Oyster crackers-those little, Saltine-like crackers that come in a small cellophane bag and are intended to be added to soup or chowder. Tasty, but full of gluten. At home, he feasted on boxes of Cheerios, which were not gluten-free as some are today. And his favorite snack of all time was the ubiquitous and yummy little orange cracker: Goldfish.

Cheerios were mostly a morning thing, though my car was loaded with them, mostly under his car seat and, interestingly, under the rear floor mat. Maybe Cheerios have a superpower of inanimate objects, but being blessed with the power of movement? My dad found Cheerios under the furniture weeks after a family visit to his condo. A visit that included our Labrador retriever, Joe! I believe that there is no bigger people-food or trash eater in the canine world as a lab so Jon must have tucked those suckers away really thoroughly.

The summer that Jon was three there were a couple of days when Jon fooled me into thinking that he'd finished his morning bagel only for me to see it floating in the ocean hours later where he had, I assumed, disposed of it earlier. Mandatory mouth checks were instituted so soggy bagel bites were not left in the ocean for the seagulls to fight over. He was nicknamed chipmunk cheeks that summer.

But this isn't about Oyster crackers, Cheerios, bagels, or clueless parenting. It's about the cheesy, salty, and delectable Goldfish cracker.

Jon could eat these by the bagful. I was even known to buy the big box, which was challenging to keep fresh in the humid Maine summer. Thanks to Jon there was very little waste, and let's be honest here-once you eat one of those salty fish it's hard to stop. I think we all consumed hundreds of those crackers for many years.

One spring when Jon was almost two, he and I ventured from Maine to Virginia to visit my mom. It was just me and Jon. Why I thought this was a good idea I'm not sure. I was wearing a wrist brace to protect and support my right wrist which sustained some joint damage due to my fairly newly diagnosed condition of psoriatic arthritis. I was also dealing with luggage and, because Jon wasn't yet two, he was sitting on my lap on the plane. Paying for only one seat is probably why I thought that this was a good idea in retrospect.

Mom asked for a list of preferred foods for Jon. At the top of the list was that delicious Goldfish cracker, naturally.

The visit was mostly uneventful with lots of food and sticky Popsicles, trips to the playground, and time spent with family. There wasn't much sleep because the rock star sleeper from my past had turned into a more typical, at least in my experience, wakeful toddler.

As promised, the house was stocked with Goldfish and Jon had more than his share. Food would sometimes stave off a tantrum, which I found to be a quite magical solution. We were just starting the tantrum phase so strategies to help manage these fits were still being discovered and anything that worked (not much) was magical.

On this trip, I also realized that Jon has a special love for the Grateful Dead. My stepbrother played his guitar in the Florida room and Jon hung out on the two steps that led down to that room filled with plants and ceramics, which were many years older than Jon.

Jon seemed to be just chilling on those two steps, lying down on one or the other, moving up and down, or even just sitting with a plastic bowl of Goldfish crackers. He didn't seem to be paying attention to much more than the music. He was in a trance-like state. It was a most welcomed break for me.

What became obvious when my stepbrother returned to William and Mary was that Jon was taking everything in. One day right before we were supposed to go home, Jon got away from me for a few minutes. I quickly found him in the den. It was just a few minutes later that my mother came upon a decapitated ceramic duck made by the stepbrother who so thoroughly entertained Jon with his music. She also discovered some very old and large potted plants that had been with my stepfather for many, many years, and were pretty much removed from their peaceful pots. The room was a mess in a matter of minutes!

Next to the duck head and not far from the duck body were two Goldfish crackers. Jon's way of leaving a calling card?

I was mortified and remember feeling glad that our plane was leaving the next day.

It was much later that I learned that my mom was not looking forward to explaining the demise of decades-old semi-tropical trees and a sentimental ceramic waterfowl to my stepfather.

Fair enough.

I've mentioned many times that Jon was a bolter. If he wasn't being physically restrained, then off he went. Sometimes, this wasn't too concerning, but often it was-for safety's sake, of course.

When Jon was barely walking, we had been visiting friends for dinner. We gathered our coats and started saying goodbye with promises of getting together again soon.

It was during this period of mild chaos and with a total of four boys ranging in age from three to a brand-new infant. Bobby, at three years old and being the oldest of the four, was keeping track of things. While we were all standing in the kitchen, he suddenly asked, "Mom, where's Jon?" Full-on panic ensued. It was dark and cold outside, and the door had been opened to the mudroom to gain access to coats and boots.

As far as I can guess, Jon had seen an impressive puddle in the yard when we arrived in fading daylight. Said puddle was deep from melting snow after a long winter. The ground was lower in that spot from the above-ground pool that had occupied the space the previous summer. Water naturally pooled there.

After seeing the outside door ajar, the owner of the house ran out to the yard. Jon was sitting in the puddle with water up to his chest. He was not happy to be removed by the homeowner. In fact, it brought on a full-blown tantrum. A theme that would repeat many times in the next couple of years. And scare the crap out of everyone around. We borrowed some clean and dry clothes and made a mad dash to get our little family home. What could have happened dominated the adult conversation on that 30-minute ride.

Those plans to get together ended up being years in the making.

Another time, we were at a camp on a lake visiting with other friends. They were there with a brand-new baby, their only child: another boy. This was only a couple of months later, but the weather was nice and warm with no puddles in sight.

I sat with Jon on a blanket near the lake. I was admiring the new baby. Jon, it seemed, was scheming. From where I sat, I had a very clear view of the small sandy beach. I felt that between sitting with Jon and keeping an eye on the most obvious point of entry to the seductively cool lake water, that I was in good shape to keep him safe.

Before long I heard another, "Mom, where's Jon?" This time he was in the lake. No one saw him scramble over the woody shoreline where Joe, the dog, had been swimming. What we did see was an 20-month-old treading water. When he was 'rescued' by Dave, he screamed bloody murder. The parents of our friends were so scared that we all thought they would have heart attacks. That was the end of that visit and any future visits to that lake. Again, thoughts of what could have been dominated the ride home.

The next week I went to the town swimming pool to see about signing Jon up for private swimming lessons because he was way too young for group lessons at that point. I was told that he wouldn't have the muscle memory to learn to swim at such a young age. I did some 'mommy and me' classes with him, but that was such a struggle because he was always trying to get away from me and made learning anything almost impossible. Plus, he was so far beyond the other kids. He loved to have his head dunked into the pool water. No need to blow into his face to make him hold his breath. He already had that trick.

Finally, I got the pool director to agree to some private lessons with two instructors-for safety's sake. I couldn't stay in the bleachers to watch because his behavior was better without an audience made up of mom and Bob. He had already learned to tread water. He still doesn't swim typical strokes but is more than capable of getting himself across a pool or lake.

Jon's style is a bit unorthodox. He still likes to swim out over his head and tread water. He then goes underwater and pops back up to grab some air. When he pops back up, I never know if I will see an arm or a leg. A hand or a foot. He sometimes lets out a squeal of delight as he does this. He disappears under the water again and pops back up with a different appendage and another squeal. I call this his 'Jaws' act as it really does look like he's being eaten by a Great White. The first time I saw this behavior was at a local, indoor pool.

The chance of a shark was extremely low.

It was easier to watch than when he took his show to the ocean where real sharks reside.

When my adorable boys were still young and very cute, I was obsessed with chronicling everything with my old Kodak. Bobby was most often the one to hold his brother in the frame. Sometimes, it looked like Jon was trying to escape from his brother's grasp; he was. Sometimes it looked like Bobby was going to hurt Jon; he never did. A similar pose with Bobby trying to look casual with his brother in what might eventually turn into a headlock was repeated time and time again. It was repeated at home for several Christmas photos. My favorite was of my toddler boys sitting in front of the fireplace, wearing white button-down shirts, khaki pants, and red bow ties. I think I started with the dog in the picture, but that particular day I gave up on the trio. Bobby was doing his best with his arm around Jon. Jon was squirming and had started to cry. Bobby was getting frustrated and I'm sure both boys were getting warm sitting on the hearth; protected by a screen from the roaring fire behind them. It was early September and still quite warm in Maine.

I shot an entire roll of film over the course of 30 minutes or so. At one point, Jon was full-on crying and trying to wiggle away and Bobby was scowling. By the end, I think all three of us were crying. In, what I can only describe as a minor Christmas miracle, I was rewarded with one decent shot the next week when I went to CVS to pick up the 48 images: Doubles, of course.

The photo that was never taken but is burned into my mind is classic and cherished. We were in church on Christmas Eve and the boys were wearing their white shirts and red bow ties again. My dad was with us; dressed in a blue blazer with gray wool slacks. His shock of full white hair was impeccably combed, as usual. I was sitting in the middle with a child on each side and an adult (my dad and Dave) flanking the ends in the pew that we shared with other young families. I have no idea what I was wearing-it didn't matter-this wasn't about my clothes. Somehow, both boys fell asleep leaning on either side of me. The chaos of trying to get two small boys fed, cleaned, and dressed for church had been forgotten during this blessed nap. The anticipated arrival of their beloved Grampy, probably caused them to miss their naps earlier in the day. Since it was Christmas Eve, we had to get to church early to even get a seat. It was an early mass especially arranged for young families. Preparations began at 2 PM. I am so happy to have such a peaceful memory. I'm sure that I didn't dare move, sing, or even breathe loudly-anything that would upset that beautiful moment.

Christmas card photos were a big thing in the '90s and I was not to be denied!

Dave, Ellie
Bobby and Jon

I have a Christmas card picture taken on the front steps with the blue door and a big green wreath with a bigger red bow in the background. Same subjects. Again, or still, toddlers. Fewer tears, and probably more snacks, to keep Jon happy. I was getting the hang of this Christmas card photo thing! Bobby was on the other side of Jon in this one-to mix things up, but he still had his arm securely around his brother. They had their legs straight; sticking out instead of bent. Jon's legs were too short to reach the brick step. The bottom of their Keds showing.

One Christmas card picture of the boys sitting on the piano bench went well enough. So much so that while shooting the roll of film I missed seeing Jon jump up, but I do have a picture of him standing on the white ivory keys of the upright Steinway that I inherited from my grandmother. I haven't played since my third piano teacher dropped me in the seventies.

Piano was never my thing.

There is also the Christmas card picture of the boys on a bridge that's part of a rail trail in the woods in autumn. The golden leaves are radiating in the sunlight. Bobby was wearing his high school letter jacket and was close to a foot taller than Jon (genetics, again). He has his arm slung casually around his brother's shoulder. Only his fingers gripping that shoulder would give away that this was not two neuro-typical boys. Both smiles were forced-this game was coming to an end. Neither wanted to humor mom any longer for holiday photos.

One Christmas I took a picture of my dad and Bobby. Not for the purpose of a Christmas card. They were sitting on a white wicker loveseat that was the only den furniture we had at the time. In the corner, there was a display of huge Magnolia leaves that my mom sent up from Virginia. I had spray-painted them gold for the holiday season. Bobby and Grampy both had Christmas ties on with blue blazers and khakis. A solid blue button-down for Bobby and a blue striped one for the older Bob (Grampy). Both were smiling. Dad also sported a red vest for the Christmas Eve mass that we were planning to attend. Dad has his right arm outstretched and to the side with his open hand inviting Jon into the fold. Dad was looking toward Jon who was, in this case, outside the frame.

Professional photos seemed to be a little easier. Probably because I couldn't meltdown.

At the end of our very first professional family photo, Jon stuck his head in the cold Atlantic. We wanted a photo of our little family for Christmas gifts. We had the two boys and our Labrador, Joe. The two cats, not being beach animals, were not included. I color coordinated our look. White shirts and chinos for the adults. A bit more color for the kids. The dog remained black. We had moved to Cape Elizabeth, Maine the previous June, and wanted a picture in our seaside community. We set up near the dunes and arranged adults in back-each with a small boy in front. I had a grip on Jon. The dog was lying in front of us all. Our photographer was very patient and took rolls of film. The boys were in agreeable moods but didn't really want to sit still for too long. At the end, our photographer told us to act naturally, and she'd get some candid shots. It was in a candid shot that Jon decided to cool off by putting his head in the ocean. He bent at the waist and just put his head right in-legs hip-width apart and straight. Bobby decided that it looked fun and tried the same. His longer legs and lesser degree of flexibility didn't allow for the same pose, so he widened his stance and stuck his head into the softly ebbing water in the protected cove. The dog was running around chasing a stick into the ocean, but still in the frame. This is the picture that I kept for us. I felt like it showed the joy in our little family. This was before we knew that Jon was just a bit past quirky. Our photographer did get a decent shot, and that, more professional-looking photo, was the one we ordered for our parents as gifts. For years, Jon was comforted to see the same pic at different places when he went to visit his grandparents. He would walk right up to that photo, whether it was in Virginia, Connecticut, or Maine, and tap on the glass. My mom lived in a big house on a river near the Chesapeake Bay in

Virginia, my dad in a condo in Connecticut, and my in-laws in a small ranch in central Maine. I think that photo gave him consistency and comfort.

Maybe, he appreciated being in the frame, after all.

Two things that were obvious at a very young age are that Jon loved a good long car ride, and he has definite opinions on music. He still does love a ride and doesn't always understand if his housemates at his group home might need to use the house van for other purposes. The destination is unimportant. The global pandemic has not helped this issue.

Back when I was in high school, the New Rhythm and Blues Quartet (NRBQ) was a favorite band of mine, and "Ridin' in My Car", was a favorite song. My friends and I would cruise around our little suburban town singing at the top of our lungs.

I never said I was cool.

Jon has long had a love of cruising and music.

My guy.

When Jon was very young, he did have some signs of autism and in fact, he still does have autism, but when he was young we were holding off on any labeling so we just treated the quirky symptoms for a few years

When Jon was small and still in a car seat, he sat on the passenger side in the back. This was so that I could see him in my rearview at all times. This also meant that my rearview wasn't really giving me a good picture of what was going on outside of my car, but I adjusted.

Jon chose to sit in the same seat when he was older because I believe, that's where his car seat was when he was a small, but active, child with autism. It seems that others have refused to chauffer him and make him sit up front. Bobby, being one of these, is bigger than both Jon and me so he can dictate rules that I choose to let slide.

There was that one time when Jon was actually still using the car seat in the rear passenger position. We lived in Maine and didn't have a garage at the time. I was driving a VW Jetta, which I loved, except for its occasional tendency for all the doors to freeze solid. This happened one morning when Jon was two. I couldn't put him down on the driveway while I wrangled with the doors, trying to get one to open for me because Jon would take off running down the driveway. I did discover, with Jon on my hip, that all four doors were frozen. It presented quite the quandary. I'm sure that I asked three-year-old Bobby to hold on to his brother while I did a deeper dive into what was going on. I don't remember the exact details, but I do remember that I managed to get the front passenger door open somehow. Success.

Not really the success I had thought. I took Jon and tried to get him to go in through that front door and, ultimately in my mind, get him to climb, peacefully, into his car seat in the back. Jon has always been quite ambulatory, so I wasn't asking him to do anything that would be scary or out of his wheelhouse. It was like an old comic strip where a cat would refuse to do something an owner wanted. Actually, it was like owning that stubborn cat-Jon put all four limbs out and refused to let me 'help' him through that front seat door. By this time, we were, most certainly, late for wherever we needed to be on that freezing winter day. At least two of us were crying. Bobby may have been able to hold it together.

Ultimately, I did not have to wait for spring to come to resume normal driving activity. I must have put the three-year-old in the house with the two-year-old and strict instructions to keep Jon out of the bathrooms, fridge, cellar, and anywhere else he might like to go, and, most importantly, to not let him get completely undressed. This last point was especially important as naked was his preferred state.

My plan was to climb through the passenger side front seat and wedge myself in the back, positioned between two car seats. Next, I pulled on the handle while kicking the door open. Not the easiest feat with those two car seats. I got into position and grabbed the handle. Nothing. I forgot that the safety lock was on and could only be disabled by opening the door from the outside. It was then that I remembered the de-icing spray, which was in the glove box- not the best idea, but since one door was already open it worked for us. This new information made getting the door open, and most importantly, getting access to that rear passenger side car seat much easier. I'm pretty sure that we didn't actually go anywhere that day-already being so late for whatever our plans were.

Did Jon win? Did I win? Does it matter?

Car rides have always been soothing for Jon and he is almost always happy to get in the car. Part of his routine is to be in charge of the radio. This would seem tricky being non-verbal and from the back, passenger seat, but he still manages to indicate music that he deems in poor taste. Peripheral vision is important when driving, but especially important when driving with Jon. He jabs his left pointer finger toward the radio, which is, in every car that I've owned, in the front seat. When he was very young, I didn't always see the jabbing finger so he might add a grunt or groan to get my attention. I would either change the radio station or advance the tape or CD until I landed on something that suited him. He still has strong musical preferences and living with four other young adults with intellectual disabilities has opened his world to country music. As an adult, he has a very eclectic musical palette ranging from The Grateful Dead, Bonnie Raitt, The Backstreet Boys, and some country. There is nothing like hearing your 29-year-old son giggling to, "I Want it That Way."

When the boys were both toddlers, I took them to Portland to hear a band that was playing outside at a local rock radio station. We drove across the Million Dollar Bridge, which has since been replaced by a much more expensive and larger draw bridge. It was always exciting if a tanker was coming up the Fore River. That day there was no tanker and we sailed right into the city and scored a prime parking spot.

It was The J. Geils Band who I had seen several times in high school and college. I was planning a trip down memory lane and thought introducing the boys to live music was a great idea. It was outside and free and a beautiful spring day. We hung out in the back of the crowd because I wasn't keen on losing my two small boys that day. The band was on a balcony so I could still see the band and there was no trouble hearing them. At all. The band played a short set, and I had a quick trip back to my carefree high school days.

Bobby was in a mood and sat on a curb around a monument with his back to the band-arms crossed over his little chest. He was extraordinarily verbal at a very young age but chose non-verbal communication to show me his displeasure that day. Jon, in a tiny jean jacket, on the other hand, seemed captivated. He let me hold his small hand and didn't try to get away from me. Not even once. It was a magical day. Jon tends to follow my musical taste.

Bobby listens to rap.

Living with, and caring for, a child with autism can present many challenges. I didn't know that he had autism when he was only two, but I did know that other moms had different challenges than I. I would often find myself in situations where I couldn't find quite what I needed for whatever reason.

It might have been as simple as finding the perfect movie that would allow me to have a few quiet moments to myself on occasion. As you may know, Disney has a pretty good formula down where they get through most any story in 90 minutes. Disney also did this thing back in the '90s where they only released a movie on VHS tapes for a short amount of time before they put it in the vault only to re-release it a number of years later. Not sure if this is still a thing without a need for Disney VHS tapes to play in the VCR that I no longer own. This vault plan did not work particularly well for us back in the days of VCRs, and subsequently, broken VHS tapes. I had an army of people always on the lookout for used copies of "Beauty and the Beast", "Aladdin" and "101 Dalmatians". Bless my yard sale-loving mother-in-law and friends whose children outgrew these movies and who would donate to our cause. If you know anything about autism then you probably know that "The Lion King", as good as it may be, is a poor replacement for "101 Dalmatians", which was the number one film in my world at that time.

Nobody puts Baby in a corner.

Except for Cruella Deville. She can do that.

It wouldn't surprise me if Bobby can still recite these three movies, word for word, to this day. So, maybe I did use them for more than the occasional quiet moment. Looking back, I'd call them a daily necessity.

Another special talent of Jon's is his spot-on sense of direction. This goes back to when he was very young. Autism is all about routine and I provided that for Jon by going to the gym for two hours every morning. It was absolutely about providing routine for Jon and not about the free daycare and glorious two-hour break for me. I had to travel about 15 minutes to get to this wonderful, life-preserving, place for my two-hour holiday, at least on a good day, a day without Jon melting down, it was two hours. I would drive the same route every morning. Under the train tracks, hoping to see a train, and then past the UPS distribution facility. Bobby was in a UPS phase and very excited about the dispatch of so many brown trucks at the same time, just after 9 am five days a week. After about a year of this, Bobby went to pre-school so I would drop him off two mornings a week and continue on my way with just Jon. This alarmed Jon at first when we would detour our route under the train tracks to drop off his brother. This is when I first discovered that he was paying way more attention to our route than I was giving him credit for. Once I figured this out, I started changing up the route as much as I could because I didn't want him to get too stuck in a rut. It was uncomfortable for him, but, ultimately, he adjusted. Later I also had to adjust my route to Sugarloaf to avoid the beckoning and seductive golden arches that were the last possible stop before arriving at the mountain an hour later. Jon was known to eat his French fries with great abandon and even swiped some off unsuspecting patrons' trays. Definitely a place to avoid.

When Jon was 18-months old he was still not really talking. He had a couple of words, but he couldn't string two together. He could say things like cookie and train, but he couldn't tell me what he wanted or needed. I don't think that there is a cookie train, but how fun would that be? Jon would have loved that!

To be honest, though, I might be overplaying the train thing. Sometimes, on the way to the gym, we were rewarded with a train rumbling over us on those tracks. Every time we went under that trestle I would say the word train, while Jon said it once. In his entire life. I was at twice a day for five days a week times 50 weeks a year for two years.

I had him 5,000 to one.

And I don't even do math!

The one thing that Jon could do, verbally at that time, was count. He could count to twenty very clearly. One day I was chatting with a mom at Bobby's preschool and tiny Jon, wearing his Osh Kosh (by gosh!) pinstriped overalls was quietly counting to twenty as he held on to my pant leg. The other mom looked at me quizzically and I remember saying that Jon was my little engineer. We laughed. Train conductor engineer. Math and science, MIT educated engineer. It didn't really matter and wasn't really that funny-even without his later diagnosis.

At the time, I didn't realize that Jon had autism. I had one son who spoke very early. In fact, Bobby made me laugh when he was nine months old and saw the tabloids lined up at the grocery checkout. As I unloaded the groceries to the belt, he pointed to one of the covers and clearly said, "Oprah." It was then that I realized that I had to switch back to Sesame Street while making dinner. My little sponge child was probably picking up more than I realized while I cooked. Perhaps because Bobby was so verbal at such a young age and because all the advice to young moms is to not compare your kids, I wasn't too worried about Jon's lack of verbal skill- yet. Plus, I couldn't help but notice every day how different they looked. Surely their different genes would produce different abilities. Bobby was always happy to interpret for Jon and I seemed to know what Jon wanted or needed before he did, so it wasn't terribly hard to deal with his lack of communication at this stage.

As I later learned, counting by rote is common for kids with autism. Maybe not counting, but learning by rote, for sure. For Jon, the counting, and where I suspect he learned it, went back to when he was a tiny baby. I would carry him upstairs and count each step. Thirteen. I would count as I dressed him. One sock, two socks-you get the picture- why I did this I have no idea. I didn't do it with Bobby, but it was just a thing I did with Jon.

Shortly after this counting moment at Bobby's pre-school, Jon went silent. By this, I mean that he didn't speak at all for about 18 months until he was around three years old. He wasn't technically silent because this was the point where he picked up tantrumming. He would have five or six episodes of trantrumming each day and these episodes would last for around twenty minutes. Each. The high-pitched noises that came out of that child were truly deafening and I was very sad for our big black Lab with sensitive dog hearing. I would use counting to try to stem the tantrums, and it distracted him for a few seconds, but often they just had to run their course.

When Jon came out of the tantrumming phase, which at the time seemed like a true miracle, his perfect pronunciation was gone, but his ability and need to count remained.

Counting is still soothing to Jon. It's probably the rote part that he likes. The predictability of what comes next. Jon has seizure disorder. The seizures started around puberty, and I won't bore you with the details, but routine blood work is a part of his, and often my, life. He hates it. For the record, I do, too. At one point we were doing drive-through blood draws. I drove up to the valet parking section of the hospital, in my SUV, with teenaged Jon, wearing a T-shirt, in the front seat. Dave in the back. I buzzed down his window and locked it in the open position and Dave leaned over Jon and held him still-his right arm sticking out the window his bare arm clad only in a tee shirt. Three phlebotomists came out to collect the necessary vials while I sat on Jon's lap to prevent him from escaping his father's hold. As I've mentioned he was ridiculously strong. We did this in January. In Maine. There is a special place in heaven for those phlebotomists. The lovely trio of women who still team up to draw blood from Jon have learned to count with me to distract Jon from the invasive needle that probably doesn't hurt but is so very distressing to him. Eventually, we moved inside to the lab, but planned physical restraints by me are still part of the deal.

And candy.

Starburst.

Jon will never be an engineer, but he does still appreciate the rhythm of numbers.

I am in no way an engineer either, but the idea that I thought was so very, very clever was in response to Jon's naked phase. Both boys always wore the footie PJs to ward off the Maine chill, especially, but not only, in the winter. This was fine for quite a period of time and continued to be fine for Bobby. For some unknown reason, Jon began to undress in the evening after his bath. Perhaps the freeing nakedness of the bath was something that he just wanted to extend into the night. In any case, he would often take off his cute footie PJs and sometimes his diaper and run through the house with abandon. This was problematic mostly after he was in his room for the night. To combat this, we cut the feet off his PJ's and then put the PJ's on backward so that the zipper went up his back and was harder for him to reach. It was sometime around age three or four when this all began. I was so proud when this worked. For two nights. He walked around the house with a green sleeper with a purple dinosaur. On his back. No problem for Jon. Not so quick to give up, I devised a better plan. I took a cloth diaper safety pin in a pretty pastel color that had a safety cover and a cute little animal on top. I liked these pins because I thought that there was less chance of Jon stabbing himself in the back of his neck and they were nice and big and easy to work with. I would insert the pin into the hole in the zipper tab and pin the zipper tab to the neck of his jammies. This kept his pajamas on for another two days. It became a battle of wills that I was determined to win. My next idea was to use a small piece of duct tape, which I would wind around the head of the pin. This would completely disable him from getting that pin undone. It also greatly hindered me from efficiently changing his diaper. That sticky tape residue was forever ruining my manicures!

The real reason for the necessity of this last invention was Jon's delight in playing with his own excrement after releasing himself from his dirty diaper. For whatever reason, Jon would do his usual bedtime routine: bath, teeth, squirming away from me in his closet as I tried to read to him. This last thing was abandoned after I realized that my crying while trying to read to Jon who was only interested in getting away from me wasn't doing either of us any good.

Once alone, Jon would relieve himself of whatever was in his bowels and proceed to get out of that diaper. I remember one time hearing him roaming upstairs. I went to check and there was a dirty diaper on the wooden stairs halfway between the first second floors. If you've ever used a disposable diaper, you might remember that wet diapers turn into lots and lots of little balls that, magically, absorb the moisture. These little balls were stuck to the ceiling of the stairway, and the walls, and the stairs, but the ceiling proved most problematic as far as cleaning goes.

Because he was a bolter/roamer I had to lock him into his room at night. This was mostly for his safety, but it also provided some peace of mind to me as well as some much-needed rest. The lock was a deadbolt installed at the top of the door so that Jon couldn't reach the lock and turn the bolt. The keyed side of the lock was on the outside and the keys were left in the lock for quick access and safety reasons. The lockdown didn't stop at his bedroom door. We also had these locks (installed) properly on the outside doors of both houses, (our main house and later our mountain house), so that Jon couldn't escape. There was the time when I was upstairs drying my long hair and my neighbor called to tell me that my toddler boys were wrestling in the driveway. I ran down to find Bobby dragging Jon back into the house. Apparently, Jon had plans somewhere else in the neighborhood-a busy guy with places to go. High locks became a necessity.

After the nightly lockdown, Jon would remove the dirty diaper and paint himself and the walls with his own fecal matter. It was really quite disgusting and not the thing anyone wanted to face every night at 10 before going to bed. He especially liked to put his poop in his ears. His face looked like he was wearing some odd war paint. Back into the tub, he would go. Dirty clothes and faded sleeping bags went directly into the washing machine with lots of bleach and bypassing the laundry chute. Even, light sleeper Bobby would be in Jon's doorway with a roll of disinfectant wipes.

One time I walked into the room, and he had used his poop and his hand to make a perfect circle of little handprints on his bare wall. I didn't know whether to cry or take a picture. If I had an iPhone like I do today, I might have done both. As it stands, there is no photographic evidence of this event, but it is surely burned onto my brain.

The hardest part might have been thinking that I'd solved the problem, which I did for about two nights after each modification. In the end, and before he outgrew this nasty phase, he was pulling the dirty diaper out through the leg hole and accessing his poop that way.

Clearly, I'd been defeated.

It would be many, many years before Jon was fully toilet trained, but at least he gave up playing with poop.

Determined doesn't even begin to describe him at that frustrating stage that only lasted a couple of months. A long couple of months, for sure.

Maine winters are cold and snowy. Caribbean cruises are (usually) warm and sunny.

Before Jon was actually diagnosed with autism Dave and I had an opportunity to go on a short Caribbean cruise that he earned through work. There would be other associates from his company on that cruise and lots of adult company and fun in the sun. I was desperate to make this cruise happen. Two toddlers and a black lab was a big ask. Who could I ask? Who would say yes? My mom was still working in Virginia. My dad was in Connecticut and always ready to help, but this seemed too much for him. My mother-in-law was semi-retired, lived an hour away, and had spent a lot of time with the kids. She agreed.

We eagerly packed our bags and made plans. It was only a three-night cruise, so it wasn't too hard to pack. It took much more time to write out pages of instructions and notes. This was before Jon was taking meds for behavior and sleep, so I didn't have to worry about a long med list with detailed instructions. Still, the kids had schedules. Jon, with his therapies, more so than Bobby, but Bobby did have occasional playdates.

My mother-in-law came the night before our morning flight to Florida. I briefed her on the kid's schedules and Jon's current antics. He liked to switch things up when it seemed like I might get ahead of him and ruin his fun. I tucked the kids in and prepared for my few days of adult conversation and no changing diapers.

The cruise was heavenly. We did all the things that people do on cruises. I guess. This was our first and only. We enjoyed the sun and went on shore excursions in the Bahamas. We watched the shows at night. And we ate. And we drank. It was a nice getaway that was over before we knew it.

When we returned to our house, the first thing we saw was my mother-in-law's suitcase packed and by the back door. This wasn't a good sign. She and the kids and dog came to meet us. Then she left. We thought she might stay the night and leave in the morning, but she was eager to get out of there.

I walked from the kitchen into the dining room, catching her car leaving the driveway through the window. The dining room table was where we left it. All six chairs were pulled away from the table. I thought that this was curious in my post-cruise haze. It was about two seconds later when my brain kicked in that I noticed that the light in the room seemed just a bit different. the chandelier didn't usually sit two inches off the table. That day it did.

I guess that I forgot to mention to my mother-in-law that Jon had started trying to get onto the dining room table and swing the gold six-armed chandelier that hung with a big gold chain from the ceiling.

I never did mention this incident to my mother-in-law. I have no idea if she knew that it happened. She did continue to visit us and would occasionally watch the kids for a couple of hours, but we never did ask her for overnight care again.

Later, I would discover respite care. These trained respite workers were lifesavers when I had to go out of town.

I'm sure that my mother-in-law appreciated them as well.

Balance was something that came easily to Jon.

The rocky soil in Maine makes for lovely stone walls surrounding the houses-especially near the rocky coast. It's my understanding that those rocks often came from the soil when the foundation for the house was dug. In any case, the house we lived in had a rock wall across the backyard and down the side of the property. This was a natural barrier for wandering toddlers and sometimes a haven for snakes and chipmunks who liked to hide out and avoid young toddlers. The natural barrier worked for a while, but Bobby often had to hop over the wall, which was probably only a foot tall, to chase errant Wiffle balls into neighboring yards. Jon, on the other hand, didn't so much climb over these walls as he preferred to run along them. He was semi-contained and never alone out there.

What makes this interesting is the fact that these walls were made of irregular-sized and shaped rocks that were not, in any way, attached to each other by cement or any other compound. They were stacked on top of and next to each other. Jon would start in the corner at the huge oak tree with the red rope swing that gently beckoned and run to the neighbor's wooden fence. It wasn't super far, but it did require balance as the rocks would skitter and skatter under his little blue, (or white or red) Keds. How he did this without falling is a mystery to me, but he did it quite often. Bobby and his friends would, occasionally, give it a try, but none had the method down quite as well as Jon.

This rock running became more serious when Jon went down to Two Lights State Park to work on motor planning as part of his occupational therapy by running on the big uneven rocks with crevices that could easily grab and twist an ankle.

This is an activity done by many; hopping from one rock to the next, occasionally stopping to look for crabs in the tidal pools created by the ebbing sea. These rocks head from the grassy picnic area down to the crashing waves. There is no beach here. Jon wasn't very interested in the crabs, but he was always pushing the envelope by trying to get down to the wet rocks, which have barnacles, and sometimes slippery seaweed, on them. We had the same perilous experience when walking out to the end of the jetty in Kennebunkport, but he loved it so. This was especially exciting at low tide when the drop to the river or ocean, depending on which side of the jetty he ran, was quite far. I didn't allow him to run amok, but I did have to work hard to keep up. He was very stable and very curious.

I was just in for the ride.

I'm not sure how important McDonald's playlands are to moms today, but back in my day, they were a big part of life.

The fries weren't bad, either.

Jon, with his exceptional balance, loved to climb to the top of the slide at those indoor fun houses provided by Ronald McDonald. Occasionally or eventually, depending on the day, Jon would even slide down to have a bit of lunch.

I knew where all the best McDonald's, with the best playlands, were up and down the East Coast from Maine to Virginia and back. These researched and planned stops got our family from Portland, Maine to Newport News, Virginia in a grueling 13 hours.

Leave at 3 AM, clear Hartford by six, stop for breakfast, and an energy release break at a playland before tackling NYC. Exercise again in NJ, lunch in MD, (at, you guessed it-Mickey D's). Stop again in Virginia and arrive at my mom's around 4 PM. Adults completely worn out; kids ready for the real playground at the end of her street.

Jon loved to climb so much that it got to the point where I had to avoid even driving by a playland in order to prevent a meltdown. Since we both learned about behavior modification at his special pre-school for kids with autism, I had to pay attention and save the rewards for when they were earned rather than cause a new set of unpleasant behaviors.

It's a delicate balance.

PART 2
THE EARLY SCHOOL YEARS

It all started with a hearing test. I knew that Jon wasn't hard of hearing because we often were out in the yard which was in the flight path for the Portland Jetport at that time. He would look up before anyone else could hear a plane. There was always a plane coming when he did that. He just heard it first. He could also hear me pop the top of a can of Coke from up in his room on the second floor when I was downstairs in the kitchen. My guilty pleasure was also a favorite drink for toddler Jon. I couldn't get away with anything.

There were two women working when Jon had his hearing test. One ran the controls and the other watched his eye movement. Through this method, they confirmed that Jon could hear. He was just not responding to my voice or the world around him. They gave me some info on an agency for services. This was a scary time and hard to take as a parent.

We knew that Jon had something going on but held off the actual diagnosis in an effort to not label him. He still received all the same services as a child with autism, we just didn't label until he was of pre-school age and, often, we private paid for services such as occupational, speech, and play therapies. This was before birth-age three services were available in Maine through the agencies. Starting services at three isn't exactly early intervention, but as I mentioned, Jon started before he was two.

Jon developed fairly normally for the first year. He did some things that I thought quirky, but not enough to think twice about. He would line all his, (hundreds), of Match Box cars on the orange shag carpet that we hadn't had time, energy, or money to replace yet. He lined those cars up for what seemed like miles. He would line them bumper to bumper-all facing the same direction. We adults came up with a game. One of us would distract him and the other 'adult' would turn one of the cars and face it the other way. He would look back and notice immediately and fix the problem. It didn't bother him that we did this, but it certainly seemed to bother him that one car was facing the wrong way. It's funny how young parents amuse themselves.

Jon lost all speech when he went into his tantrumming (my word for multiple, daily, and lengthy out-of-control tantrums) phase. This phase lasted about 18 months and he would tantrum for 15 to 20 minutes several times a day. I would try to hold him to console him. He wanted none of that and would stiffen his body and slither out of my grasp. The screams right next to my ear were so painfully loud and piercing that I just let him go. I don't remember much from those months. He had other classic signs of autism like arm flapping and toe walking. Seemingly, benign enough on their own. He was also not at all interested in any other kids and was lost in a world of his own. There are very few pictures from this stage of Jon's development.

At age three he was funded for services based on a diagnosis from his doctor of Pervasive Developmental Disorder. At four Dave and I went to Boston for the eventual and unsurprising diagnosis of Autism. His behaviors were increasing, but his speech was not. The autism diagnosis allowed him to qualify for the funding for his second year of pre-school. I went through the Kubler Ross stages of grief. Bargaining was a place where I got stuck a lot. It would be years and lots of hard work before I found acceptance. When I was a journalism student in the early 1980's I had a class that required me to *peruse* the entire Sunday New York Times. I *skimmed* an article on autism and thought that "I really don't know what that even means". In a time before Google or even Ask Jeeves I decided that I really didn't need to know more about autism. In one way I was correct. That article was not discussed in class that week. In a more important way, I was very wrong. I'm less cavalier about dismissing things that might be important.

When Jon was five, he attended the May Center in Portland, Maine. This special pre-school for students with autism was very expensive and was, luckily, covered by his federal funding for children diagnosed with intellectual disabilities. It was also very intense!

Students arrived at school in a desirable section of Portland. I think it's a restaurant now, but that's not important. Four and five-year-old's from all over the greater Portland area were brought in by mom or dad for a full day of learning and behavior modification. These were the same children who couldn't sit still for two minutes and suddenly, they were expected to sit at long worktables from 9-3 PM, five days a week. There were some meltdowns, small acts of violence, and, eventually, some behavior modification. Jon pulled the fire alarm twice. It was all very exciting, I'm sure. I was told that he had used two of his three strikes. Somehow, he never did it again. Learning to pee in a toilet was a behavior that I was especially thankful for!

The day this process started, we arrived at school before the other kids. 8:30 sharp and armed with salty snacks and a 2-liter bottle of ginger ale. This doesn't seem like sound parenting, but I was desperate to ditch the multiple diapers and pull-ups each day. Jon happily ate his salty snacks and drank as much soda as he pleased. Staff traded off taking him to the bathroom every 15 minutes to sit for five and hope some pee landed in the toilet. The reward for this was gummy bears. I recall it taking most of the day, but eventually, Jon got the hang of it. We weren't quite out of the woods yet, though.

The move from pull-ups to big boy underwear was greatly celebrated by all. Except Jon. He liked to have very small accidents that would result in a time out. He liked this because he was getting the attention from whomever he desired with this pesky behavior. He never had a full-on accident, but just enough to wet his pants a bit. One weekend day I stopped counting at 12 time-outs. I could get nothing done because Jon wasn't keen on staying in his time-out spot, so I had to watch him sit. This was way before we had phones to play with while waiting.

That Monday morning, I spoke with the director of his program. Jon was with us, but seemingly not listening. He had this attention-seeking behavior at school as well, so I totally had the director's attention. She had suggested a device that could be somehow inserted in his underwear to detect wetness. He undoubtedly heard this conversation and I'm happy to say that was all it took to get this behavior to stop.

Bowel training came many, many long years later, but at least he only wore his pull-ups at night and never did return to the dreaded playing with poop phase,

The May Center was also pretty instrumental in helping Jon change his footwear as his feet grew. They also taught him how to tie his shoes. Jon, ever the opportunist, would allow anyone to tie his shoes as long as he didn't have to do it himself. Some twenty-odd years later as I watched a Direct Support Professional tie his shoes I asked, "You do know that he can do that, right?" He had no clue. Being a mean mom, I had Jon show him right then and there.

Change is hard. It can be especially hard for children with autism. In Maine, we are lucky to enjoy the beautiful four seasons. I mention this because with season changes come clothing changes. It was always hard to watch as Jon transitioned from chilly spring to full-blown summer. This could happen in one day in Maine! He would constantly, and unsuccessfully, try to pull his short-sleeved shirts down over his forearms because he was used to having them covered for the prior nine months. Long pants to shorts were equally tough to watch. I've noticed that his group home is warm enough that he can wear shorts and a tee in the winter when he's just hanging around. He also goes to the gym a lot and has to change for that. Perhaps it's easier for him now.

Probably the biggest challenge, when Jon was young, was getting, and keeping, shoes on his feet. Jon loved to walk barefoot. In fact, the fewer items of clothing on his body the better. He was a toe-walker as a baby and all that tiptoeing around probably made shoes, which required him to keep his feet mostly flat, pretty uncomfortable. He really did prefer to be barefoot and having daily access to the beach all summer probably didn't help. Sandals, for some reason, were never, ever an option. In fact, both boys rejected them immediately upon presentation.

When Jon was young, I figured out that moving from one shoe size to the next was problematic because he liked the old comfy broken-in shoes. His feet were growing, and new shoes just felt different. I wasn't sure if it was the style shoe that was uncomfortable, so I went for a soft and more pliable canvas Keds brand sneaker. After a few years of trying to keep sneakers on growing feet, I decided that it might be best to add an element of surprise to the process. It's important to note that shoes are required at many places we frequented. The grocery store being the most important.

The May Center suggested that I buy a few pairs of Keds in his size and a few pairs in the next half size-switching up the colors, of course. Our plan was to mix up these sneakers so that Jon would never be able to anticipate which pair I presented him with in the morning. If he noticed, he didn't squawk too much. This plan actually worked for quite a few years. Either that or he just accepted wearing sneakers as part of the daily deal. Ice cream is at the grocery store and Jon loves ice cream. This may have been his compromise.

I never bought into the Velcro sneaker craze, which is kind of funny because I was a children's shoe buyer for a few years before I had my own kids. I bought all kinds of Velcro sneakers and my stores sold, literally, thousands of those cute, colorful and tiny kicks. During the process of being a shoe buyer and before I had kids of my own, I learned that Velcro, while helpful on one hand, is actually very difficult to control. As easy as it is to get into a Velcro sneaker, it's at least twice as easy to get out of one, and once it's off, it can be temporarily lost in the vast wilderness of the backseat of the car. Not to say that we didn't lose a few sneakers, back in the day. Even double-tied laces can be untied, and shoes can be kicked off. There seemed to always be a workaround for such situations as unwanted footwear.

In any case, the rotating of Keds canvas sneakers worked like a charm. Jon never did know which pair would be presented to him on any given morning. He would sometimes be sporting red and the next day they might be blue. When he was getting close to moving to the next size, I might add a pair of white ones to change things up, and, all of a sudden, we had transitioned to the next half-size and all was well. Looking back, I now realize that Zappos would have been a huge help!

This was a little harder, (OK, almost impossible and horribly expensive), to do with ski boots, but for school and the beach, my plan was gold. Winter boots were a whole different beast. I didn't stockpile them like the much smaller sneakers. He hated the heavy and confining winter boots and to this day he balks at wearing them. He will still sometimes show up for dinner in his black mesh Reeboks with a foot of snow on the ground. I've asked his group home to try to redirect him to the proper pull-on boots with a side zipper, but he will always try to get back to those black sneakers. He buys (with lots of help) his own clothes and footwear these days and I've noticed that he has eschewed any color at all in his footwear. Not so for his clothing, but certainly footwear, as he is almost exclusively wearing black Reeboks these days.

Having a child with autism has made me rethink communication. Verbal, of course, but communication in general. When Jon was at the May Center in Portland; an intense preschool for students on the autism spectrum it was clear that all his peers struggled with communication in one way or another. Because it's a spectrum there were students of many abilities at that school. By the time Jon was at this, his second, preschool, he was almost exclusively non-verbal. I remember comparing Jon with students who could speak. These students were able to ask for what they wanted but would often throw a fit if they didn't get what they wanted. It was often not appropriate to give four-year-olds candy for breakfast and a big part of communication is not just letting needs be known, but also responding appropriately. Or at least trying to learn this skill. Jon was past his trantrumming phase and behaviors weren't really, (mostly), a problem at that time.

He did have some behavioral missteps like when getting his hair cut. One of the behavior specialists came to one of his Saturday morning barbershop appointments with me to see if we could break it down and make the chore a bit easier. The barber, Steve, would open early for me so that there were no other people or excess stimuli present during the fifteen minutes it took to do a quick buzz cut-a cut he still wears to this day. I sat in the big brown barbers' chair and put small Jon on my lap. He sat facing me and I brought him into a huge bear hug. I assure you that he hated this! I held his arms down and tucked his head between my face and shoulder. Steve could get a few quick swipes before we switched sides. The back and the top were harder to brace for, but we managed to do it on a semi-regular basis. The behavior specialist noticed right away that Jon tensed up (more) when Steve put his hand on the top of Jon's head. Good information, but it made the hard job even harder; one-handed barbering is a skill probably not taught in school. The lollipop at the end was always welcomed.

The haircut is just one example of how we navigated the waters of communication in those pre-school years. There was a lot of negotiation, some begging, lots of behavior modification (gummy bears), and, occasionally, crying by all parties. I don't think Steve ever cried. In front of us, anyway. Communication is essential for just about everything. Learning along with a non-verbal autistic child gave me a new appreciation for what often comes easily.

Seemingly, even fun things can be considered behaviors.

When the kids were little, they had a grandmother who purchased Christmas presents all throughout the year. She would lovingly arrive on Christmas morning with a carload of wrapped gifts of all shapes and sizes for the two boys. This, combined with gifts from their parents and other family members, led to Jon's nightmare; a pile of work to be tackled. Gifts need to be unwrapped and to Jon, that was work.

Bobby was more than happy to excitedly tear the paper off gifts for both boys. This was OK until Jon went to the May Center.

The May Center was all about behavior modification and his lack of enthusiasm for opening gifts was a behavior that needed modifying, in their opinion. Their advice was to let Jon pace himself with the gifts, but that he have no help and eventually, open each and every one.

The year at the May Center, the boys were up bright and early, as most five and seven-year-olds are-regardless of the special day. They first discovered the unwrapped gifts from Santa and the stockings hung by the fireplace. Later, when their grandparents came, it was time to get to the serious business of unwrapping other treasures. Bobby was gung-ho and very willing to help his brother as he had in years past, but that wasn't the plan. After about 30 minutes, and after taking a picture with each and every unwrapped gift to send to distant relatives, Jon was able to take a break: Like a cat, he would play with the boxes and not the carefully chosen gifts. Bobby, meanwhile, continued with his massive mound of goodies. Throughout the day, Jon, prompted by me, would continue to open boxes of clothes and toys that he had little interest in.

He was always happy to break for dinner and Christmas Day was no exception. Delicious and decadent food like mashed potatoes with sour cream *and* cream cheese proved to be a great break from all that unwrapping.

After dinner, one set of grandparents hopped into the much lighter Subaru wagon and headed north to their home. My dad hung around, drank wine, and listened to jazz with the adults after the kids went to bed-stuffed and exhausted.

It was after bath time that year when Jon opened his final gift, but he did open each and every one of them. By himself.

He still isn't terribly interested in the whole Christmas thing, so over the years, I've done a good job lightening his load. I will often wrap up three or four things together to make it easier and quicker for all of us.

His favorite presents are still, to this day, fuzzy fleece blankets and anything tie-dyed. He's given up playing with boxes.

He still struggles with the process and will communicate this with strange guttural sounds. He usually spends his time eating the goodies from his stocking. I found peanut butter cup wrappers in the chair where he sat, two weeks after Christmas this past year. Always sneaky, that one!

While safety was always a concern raising Jon, it wasn't the only concern. There was that one time that we were at the beach on an early spring day. Jon was a bit older and less likely to swim away like when he was a toddler. It wasn't really a beach day in the sense that it was still spring, not particularly warm and a bit windy. It was the full sun and blue sky that drew us out. It had probably been a long winter (aren't they all in Maine?) and we might have been pushing the season, but to the beach, we went. With all the toys, snacks, towels, and even a chair for me on this day.

This beach is in a protected cove and has a small stream that slowly meanders from the dune grass out to sea. After a couple of hours of the boys damming the stream and other fun stuff like Jon dumping buckets of cold water onto his head, it was time to move on to another activity. I called Bobby over to help, and together we refilled the toy bag, packed the cooler, folded the chair and towels, and prepared to walk a short distance to the parking lot.

Six-year-old Bobby took the toys, and I grabbed the rest of the stuff while holding Jon's hand in my free one. Somehow, I dropped the chair and in that split second, Jon broke loose. He didn't run to the ocean as in the past. Instead, he beelined over to a woman who was transitioning from a facedown position on her towel onto her back. He delightedly straddled her waist as she was lying on her back and put his hands right on her boobs. Thank goodness he was a very cute five-year-old and small in stature. Thank goodness she laughed! I'm pretty sure that I wasn't laughing as I apologized profusely and herded my charges to the car.

After a year at the May Center, it was time for Jon to transition into public school. There were at least five students with autism in the Cape schools ahead of Jon, so I wasn't too worried about his transition. But transition being transition, everything can be more difficult than you might imagine. I don't believe that any of those kids attended the May Center, so we were coming at this from a bit of a different angle. I spoke with anyone who would speak to me about Jon's upcoming transition. Not only would he be at a different school he would only be in school in the mornings. We didn't do full-day Kindergarten back then. At least not in that town and at that time. He (and I) was used to six-hour days with occupational and speech therapy as well as swim lessons after school. I had a meeting with the Special Education Director scheduled and wanted to know what I was in for. Someone told me, "Just don't cry in front of him." This seemed like impossible advice for an emotional person, but meet we did and cry I did not.

We worked into a pretty good rhythm during the early years in Cape Elizabeth. Jon rode the same school bus as his brother and returned home at noon on his own. I was always there to meet him. Since he loved to ride, I didn't really expect a problem. It was a big step for him. It was exciting for us. His teachers were great and always had activities that Jon enjoyed-even going so far as to have the whole class sing "If you're happy and you know it," every single day! He had a super educational technician (Ed-tech) who communicated with him very well. She also had lots of creative ideas for coming up with ways to use his skills. Sorting and matching were where he excelled and still does.

We had 40 hours of in-home support each week as well as occupational and speech therapy appointments, so I certainly wasn't in this by myself. His in-home support people and there were many, would work on skills with him as well as take him out for walks, work on daily living skills such as toileting and even cooking.

We had one in-home support person who basically just played ball with Bobby in the backyard. He didn't last too long. Another showed enthusiasm on her first day and wanted to learn more about autism. I lent her several books. She never came back, and I never did get those books back. The agency that she went through apparently never saw her again, either. We did have some great support people but the pay wasn't great, and the job was hard so it wasn't surprising when they didn't stick around. This was very frustrating for me, and I imagine, confusing for Jon.

We were always looking for things that we could do as a family.

I've been a skier since I was ten. In fact, I broke my leg while skiing in Canada that first year. That was 40 plus years ago and I still ski.

Before the kids were born, Dave and I skied. A lot. We skied in Maine and out west. We were two people with two good incomes and no kids to tie us down.

When the kids were little, it seemed important to introduce them to my winter sport. This was before I realized that Jon had autism, which pretty much complicated everything.

After the kids were born, we skied one weekend a year for the first few years. This was a treat. We'd put the kids in daycare and take the slopes by storm. That first year was easy with Jon. He slept a lot and didn't give daycare much trouble. Right before he turned two years old, he began presenting with some of the characteristics of autism. Namely, he tantrummed. We had no idea why or when this unwelcome behavior would happen. Understandably, we put skiing on hold for a couple of years.

When Jon was six years old, I tried again. I called the daycare at Sugarloaf to see if they could handle Jon and his non-verbal communication and quirky behaviors. He had reduced his tantrums quite a bit by that point, so I felt hopeful.

I worked with the head of children's programming and the manager of the daycare to have a childcare worker act as a one-on-one to keep track of Jon while we skied. I remember dropping Jon off on Saturday morning with extra clothes and tons of snacks. We were staying in the same building as the daycare, so we didn't have to fully dress him for the winter weather (a process that is truly beyond description), but the snowsuit and boots made their way into his cubby for the weekend.

Around two we broke for the day and grabbed a beer at the lodge to have a last bit of relaxation before pickup at 3 PM. Bobby was in a day-long ski school program, and we momentarily thought how great it would be if Jon could learn to ski as well. Then we laughed. We knew how hard it was to simply get sneakers on his feet, his ankles stiff from years of toe walking. There was no way, we were thinking, that he'd ever allow stiff and uncomfortable ski boots to be buckled onto his feet and ankles. I had checked with daycare around lunchtime, so I knew that as of noon things were going well and that Jon had gone outside with the other kids to go sledding. Since it was before cell phones, I made a point to regularly check the whiteboards at the bottom of each lift. It's every parent's nightmare to see your name on one of those boards, calling you back to some child emergency situation. Interestingly, it was Bobby who called us via the whiteboard one chilly (OK, it was negative ten without wind chill) New Years' Day. He was fine and playing games in ski patrol when we arrived-hours later. I wasn't trained to watch the boards until this event happened. It was clear sailing for us with Jon that day.

After grabbing Bobby from his program in the base lodge, we headed over to daycare-a short stroll across the top of a bunny slope. Jon was happy and calm when we arrived. His one-on-one came to speak with us. He was trained to work with people on the autism spectrum. How lucky did this make us? In any case, he reported having a great day with Jon and asked if he could have a crack at getting Jon on skis on Sunday. I explained about Jon's stiff ankles and his possible aversion to ski boots while I mentally thought about what I would need to do to make this happen. I was thrilled to let him try.

Sunday morning, we rented gear for Jon and dropped him off with his one-one and all his stuff. Basically, it was just skis and boots as poles have never been a thing for Jon. We left him and headed to get Bobby back into ski school for another day. I checked in at lunch and learned that Jon had, in fact, allowed his one-one, to be known from here on as the miracle worker who hung wallpaper as a side gig, to get boots onto his feet. He even locked those uncomfortable boots onto slippery narrow boards and allowed the miracle worker to guide him down the bunny trail. It may not sound like much, but this was truly a breakthrough and a major event for our little family.

That afternoon we packed up all our stuff and headed two and a half hours home. Jon smiled the entire way. He was also uncharacteristically calm and focused. He slept very well that night. We weren't sure if it was the fresh air or the skiing. We didn't care.

It sounds impulsive, and perhaps it was, but we talked about that experience and within a week we had pulled our house in Cape Elizabeth off the market. We decided that we didn't need a bigger house, but perhaps we could use a condo at Sugarloaf. By August we owned that condo and were getting ready for a full season of skiing.

Jon experienced a mix of skiing with Maine Handicapped Skiing and private lessons, and he became quite the little skier. He was also very calm in the afternoons. He was a kid who would just as soon walk across the back of the couch as sit down on it. Suddenly, he sat. It was a beautiful thing. As he became a better skier, he would take whoever was following him around the mountain into the trees and on mogul trails.

Jon just needed the chance to try something that made him feel better and calm. Once he was on skis, he took it from there.

~ ❖ ~

In our first family ski photo, it was clear that Jon was not interested in standing still and posing for the camera. He had a sly devilish look on his face with a glint in his little boy eyes and at least two of us holding onto him while trying to look natural. The first ski picture was taken on the bottom of a trail at Sugarloaf Mountain; its majestic beauty, rising in the background since skiing was the one activity that we'd found that we could do as a family. It was before we wore helmets and Bobby had a silly purple jester's hat placed jauntily on his head. Jon had a more traditional ski cap that was askew-just because. I had my long dark hair blowing in the wind-no hat. I was wearing a bright red coat that I only recently donated to clear some closet space. Dave had tinted eyeglasses and a ball cap. I was holding Jon on one side while trying not to look down, but rather look into the camera. Bobby, who was next to Jon and in front of both parents, was also helping hold Jon still. This was before the digital age, so we had to wait for photos to be developed. Oh, the disappointment at times. This particular time, we were rewarded with a nice family picture with everyone looking at the camera. It's amazing to think that this was done while on skis!

After the family picture shoot, we had the photographer get one of just the two boys. This picture is actually quite funny. Bobby is looking directly at the camera with a goofy smile on his face. He had one baby tooth and one adult tooth showing. His arm is linked with Jon's, who is looking away and ready to bolt. Again, with a devilish look on his small face. Both boys had their seasons' ski passes dangling from their dark blue L.L. Bean parkas.

The photographer commented that "someone had too much sugar in his cereal for breakfast." Jon was seven and we had already been through full-day pre-school for students with autism, behavior modification, applied behavioral analysis, off-label drug trials, multiple bolting episodes, and much more. I wasn't happy with the comment, but I had to let that one go. To try to explain to the photographer would have taken too long, might not have been understood, and, most likely, would have ended without a picture at all due to the time it would have taken to explain our situation. Sometimes I just have to pick my moments to enlighten and other times I grin and bear it. An offhand comment by a photographer, who would see us maybe one more time seemed like a good time to grin and bear it.

One time on the way home from Sugarloaf Jon was playing with a bottle of windshield wiper wash in the back seat and in his car seat. Jon and Dave were the only ones in the car, and we didn't know how long he had that plastic blue bottle with very little liquid left in it in his hands. We also had no idea how he could have gotten it off the floor of the backseat while in his car seat, but we'd seen many strange things from this child, now five years old. I can barely open those bottles, but we didn't want to take a chance that he might have gotten into it. He was in a phase where he would try drinking everything including adult beverages, so off to the ER, we all went. The male nurse informed me that he really didn't know anything about autism. I wasn't really in the mood to educate. The ER doc, another young male commented, "It would be really helpful if he could talk." That comment still floors me when I think about it. The doc drew some blood and wanted to leave the needle in his arm in case he needed to administer meds after the blood gas test. Jon didn't like the idea and that might have been the longest 30 minutes of my life between waiting for the results and trying to keep that needle in his arm.

He didn't drink poison, by the way.

Back to skiing and the necessary gear to stay warm on the slopes of Maine. An invention that I conceived, (I think) and used for years until it went missing, is the mitten shirt. This was basically a fleece pullover that had ski gloves sewn on the ends of the arms. This beauty came about after losing two pretty expensive right ski mittens in one weekend! Seven-year-olds with autism can't be expected to keep track of their things. At least that was the experience at my house. After cleaning out the inventory at the on-mountain ski shop for ski mittens that fit tiny seven-year-old hands but cost the same as gloves for 30-something-year-old adults, I came to the conclusion that something needed to be done. This problem was way more involved than the knit mittens that used to be attached by a string that would rest across your back and under your coat passing through the coat sleeves that always seemed to be red. And, apparently, deadly, strangling unsuspecting toddlers according to old wive's tales. These new mittens needed to be super warm-mostly because we lived and skied in Maine.

Ski mittens, in any size, come with a pretty thick cuff. This presented a problem for this non-sewing mom. I tried hand sewing the mittens onto the fleece with an upholstery thread and needle, but this proved too much for my sore arthritic hands. I had been diagnosed with psoriatic arthritis when Jon was just 6 months old. At my worst, I had to carry him down the stairs walking backward. Step by step. It was a real eye-opener, but eventually, the medical and pharmaceutical worlds aligned, and I found some relief. Currently, I seem to be in remission with just some meds for the joint damage that occurred in the fact-finding stage of my disease.

Back to the mitten shirt.

My solution was to take the idea to a dry cleaner that did alterations. As it turned out, my psoriatic arthritis was not really the problem, this project ended up breaking a needle on an industrial sewing machine. This made me feel a bit better about my ineptitude. Still, we plugged on and eventually found that if we only sewed the top of the mitten to the cuff of the fleece, we could get a product that we could use. This allowed Jon to take the mittens off without losing them. This would seemingly be helpful in the bathroom at the lodge. Somehow, peeing had suddenly required almost complete disrobing, which made public bathrooms tricky.

This, like many quirks of autism, seemed to pop up one day and become, "a thing". Many things could pop up one day and disappear just as quickly. Some were even cyclical, like Jon's winter spitting stage that lasted for several years, but only in the winter. It was a curious and frustrating stage where Jon would start by pushing a small bit of spit between his two front teeth. His adult teeth were not quite as perfect as his tiny baby ones. In any case, he would push that spit out a bit and suck it right back in. He would do this, letting the spit get longer and longer, still sucking it back in. It was kind of amazing, and disgusting, to watch. Eventually, and after letting that spit go down to his chin, he would just spit it all out. It didn't really matter if we were in the grocery store or outside in the snow. The yearly recurrence made me dread winter for a few years! Gross, but better than the phase of poking meat packages in the grocery store and trying to eat raw meat off his finger, and in one case, the grocery store floor. Luckily, I was right on that phase, and he didn't get E. coli. But, back to the mitten shirt.

The mitten shirt was, mostly, helpful in the spring when the weather warmed enough to warrant having bare hands in the lift lines. Since Jon has never skied with poles, (I couldn't even conceive of how I'd keep track of those projectiles), he was the one that could be seen with mittens flapping on bright spring weekends. I never did try to patent this, but he does still use a version of it. We've had many different styles over the years as he's grown, but they all served the same purpose. Recently, I had a lightbulb moment when putting on my own ski gloves. The gloves that have elastic around the wrist that allow the glove to come off and dangle, but not drop. The solution was so much easier than I ever could imagine, and it makes sense that I see fewer single gloves under the chairlift these days.

This idea is someone else's patent.

When Jon was six, I heard about Biofeedback as something that could be potentially beneficial, (life-changing, even), to young kids with autism. As with every other new idea, we (still married) jumped on the bandwagon. Bobby and Dave were on their own for a few weeks.

Living in Maine, our options were limited. I explored other states and found a provider in Northhampton, Mass. She was able to take Jon on during the summer. In August. During his one-month break between summer school and the September start of the new school year. The plan was for her to see him five days a week for three straight weeks and evaluate how he seemed after the treatment.

The non-invasive treatment involved a computer and some electrodes that were attached to his head. The computer, when activated, would appear to be very similar to a PacMan game and the theory was that Jon would be able to control the game just by thinking. It was very interesting to watch and, miraculously, he did not object to the electrodes, which was exactly the opposite of how he reacted to a planned EEG just a few years later. But, again, I digress.

This treatment involved me driving three and a half hours to Northhampton on those three Monday mornings. We grabbed something to eat, (this was before he became gluten-free so we didn't have that issue to deal with). He met with his therapist for about 45 minutes-hooked up to the machine the whole time. Our goal was to find something that might calm his mind and, and this is a huge, potentially open his mind to verbal communication.

We left the treatment center after his hour appointment, which allowed me time to talk about goals and progress with his practitioner. From there, we headed 45 minutes south to Enfield, CT where my dad was living in a condo and very close to his beloved country club. We stayed with dad for the week and returned the 45-minute one-way trip every day, Tuesday through Friday to Northhampton for his daily biofeedback session. After his Friday session, I would point the car back to Maine for the weekend-only to return the next Monday morning.

The biofeedback was very calming for Jon. He didn't improve his communication skills, but the calmness was very welcome. In the beginning, I left him (and me) locked in my dad's condo and sternly told him to be good while I took a very quick shower. The first day that I did this, (I think dad was on the golf course), I came out of the shower to find popsicle sticks all over the first floor. This was distressing because the carpet was white, but Jon is still a pretty efficient popsicle eater, so the damage was minimal.

By the end of the 3rd week, Jon was able to sit on the stairs, (why the stairs I can't recall) and not move during my very quick showers. He was certainly much calmer after the biofeedback experiment in Northhampton, but he is still non-verbal some 20 years later. Sadly, we found a practitioner in Maine and could not replicate the results, so our experiment ended after less than a year. I haven't thought about biofeedback in a long time, but perhaps it's time for a re-visit.

What makes this three-week period so interesting really isn't the biofeedback, though that was pretty interesting, or the Taco Bell lunches, which were pretty tasty, but the many hours on the road.

We left Cape Elizabeth, Maine early on Monday mornings and returned during high season vacation rush hour on Friday afternoons. We were returning to Vacationland, after all!

Jon had developed a habit that he still has to this day, where he will flap his arms around in front of his face when he is happy, or excited, or even sometimes when he is agitated. I believe it all started when the kids got a copy of 101 Dalmations one Easter. Bobby would get so excited when the brown (UPS?) truck was chasing Cruella Deville. He would flap his hands around in excitement. I believe that this is the only thing that Jon ever copied from his brother. And it stuck.

For Jon.

Bobby doesn't flap anymore.

This isn't unique in the autism community, but when you are in the car on the highway for several hours each week this flapping might be interpreted by truck drivers as the sign for honking the horn used by kids on road trips for many years. The sign looks like the signer is pulling on a string with his hand in a fist. I was probably into the second week before I figured out why all the trucks that I passed were honking at me, or more specifically, the small child in the back seat on the passenger side and buckled securely into his car seat, who was flapping away with delight at all the traffic. I thought that they were letting me know that it was safe to get back into the right lane after my superior passing skills! I had so much to learn, and this only scratched the surface.

Jon's intention, I believe, was never to get the trucks to honk; in fact, I think it irritated him a bit, but he loved car rides and the honking was just part of his time on the road. He also liked it when

I passed cars and normal-sized trucks. I was happy to oblige as he enjoyed those hours in the car far more than I. That and I felt the need to speed.

The most interesting part of the whole experience was the middle weekend. We were headed to Maine, (again, Vacationland), on a Friday afternoon in the best part of the summer. We were also headed to Maine with tens of thousands of fans of the jam band, Phish, for one of their legendary concerts in Limestone, which is pretty much in the middle of nowhere and hours away from where I ran into these happy travelers. Traffic was brutal on the turnpike and Route One didn't look any better. We were just stuck in gridlock. It was a parking lot on the Maine turnpike that afternoon. Jon didn't know about Phish to my knowledge, but he was a pretty loyal Grateful Dead fan from what I could decipher from his bossy finger that he would jab toward the front seat when he didn't agree with the music choice that the radio or CD player provided. Also, the decapitated duck situation from when he was younger. He always allowed The Dead to entertain us-country music-not so much at that time. I believe that this is changing.

Who doesn't like Chris Stapleton?

So, there we were, gridlocked in traffic, all the way from the Mass. Line, all the way through the ten or so miles in New Hampshire and 40-something slow miles into Maine. All the cars on the road contained several very happy occupants anticipating a great weekend of music and whatever else. Possibly grilled cheese sandwiches? It took an extra couple of hours to get home that day, but it's hard to get too upset when everyone else on the road was having a great time: windows down, music blaring and peace signs galore. I had chilled Chardonnay waiting for me!

We got home, did our weekend routine, and hit the road again on Monday morning and what do we see? The same VW busses and peace signs, lots of people wearing tie-dye, and all the women wearing bandannas over their not too recently, shampooed hair. Yup, we were stuck, once again, in Phish traffic, but this time they were exiting the state after a weekend of music and whatever else was going on. We were just collateral damage as far as traffic goes. We were headed once again to Northhampton to see about some biofeedback.

These were some very special mom/son bonding times and I'm glad that we had the opportunity to explore the possibilities that biofeedback might provide, but as is so true with autism, it isn't the intent that matters, it's the journey along the way that provides the memories.

When Jon was small, there wasn't much that I wouldn't try to make him more comfortable: Biofeedback, off-label drugs, a gluten-free diet, play therapy, occupational therapy (OT), speech therapy, as mentioned before, and even equine therapy.

Jon began receiving OT services at age two. His gross motor skills like walking, running (bolting!), swinging, etc., were very good. I would often accompany Jon and his OT to a state park on the ocean where Jon would work on motor planning by running across the big rocks that sloped downward from the grass to meet the sea. It was the most beautiful place to work on motor planning, but a little scary as well. I made him stay on the dry rocks above the high tide line if he was running or planning. His therapist said that he was quite good at motor planning. Advanced, even. This was a blessing and a curse. His excellent balance and planning ability helped to keep him safe. These skills also were an advantage, should he desire, as he so often did, to get away from his caretaker. My own motor planning skills were honed just to keep up with him.

Equine therapy was something that I was skeptical about at first. Jon didn't particularly care for animals; we had dogs and cats that were mostly to be avoided. There were also horses boarded up the street from our house and he never seemed too interested when I would walk the boys over to have a look or slip one a carrot.

In any case, I decided to give equine therapy a try. The closest certified facility was about 30 minutes away. It was in the next town over, but this is Maine.

It's a big state.

We would head out on Saturday mornings. Mostly, it was just me and Jon, but occasionally Bobby would have to join us. I say have to because an hour in the car and another 45 minutes watching his brother walk circles in a barn was pretty boring. I get that, but it's just part of having a special needs brother. And Jon more than made up for that by attending all his brothers sporting events for the next ten years.

The first thing that Jon did when he got to the barn was put on a helmet, (not his favorite thing, but he did it), and go into a stall with staff to meet the horse. These therapeutic horses were so gentle and, generally, unruffled by the students. Jon, very reluctantly, saddled up his horse.

When it was his turn in the ring, the therapist brought the horse to the loading platform. Here a volunteer side-walker, a person who walked beside the horse for the safety of the rider, helped him into the saddle.

The therapist walked in front of the horse with the reins and called out things for Jon to do. I think she was very surprised the first time she asked him to lean to the left. He leaned over very far without falling off or holding on. Again, his balance, (and his abs) are really amazing.

Jon also liked to go fast on the horse. He never wobbled in the saddle while trotting or leaning. As it turned out, he needed two, very hard-working, side-walkers every session, where one was typical, Jon needed the extra support for safety's sake. Though I knew that he was perfectly safe they had to work with insurance and such. The sidewalkers would be red-faced from exertion when his time on the horse concluded.

After riding for about 30 minutes, Jon got off the horse and proceeded to brush down the horse before putting the horse back into the stall. Jon hated this chore, but the riding must have been enjoyable enough to keep him coming back.

It's impossible to say how much Jon missed riding when the facility informed me that they couldn't staff his Saturday sessions. The motion of the horse seemed to make him feel better, calmer. In fact, at a recent meeting, we discussed bringing equine therapy back into his life.

Giddy-up!

Another part of Jon's quirkiness was the way he dressed.

From the time Jon was an infant he always wore clothes well. By this, I mean that everything I put on him looked great. My rule was that if the outfit didn't look good on Jon then it needed to be donated to a resale shop for some other kid to try to rock. Honestly, this didn't happen often.

My control of this theory is Jon's brother, Bobby, who also looks good in clothes, but just not quite as good as Jon did as a small child. He knows it and accepts it. That's just the way things were back in the day. These days they have completely different styles.

As Jon grew older and began to develop his unique personality, as all kids eventually do, he took over the job of dressing himself. Jon was always provided with clothes that looked nice, were comfortable, and were often purchased separately with the idea that they needn't be worn together. He was not wearing Garanimals. Both boys were usually dressed in a preppy style that included button-down oxford shirts and chinos. Nothing too fancy here. Definitely my style and not theirs. Both have since eschewed the preppy style. Jon went through an 'inside out and backward' phase, where he would wear his tee shirt inside out and backward. Clever name for that phase. I think that this inside out and backward phase was just sheer laziness on his part. Perhaps, the laziness was on my part as I, undoubtedly washed the clothes inside out which was the state that they were sent down the laundry chute in the upstairs bath. I really can't speak to the whole backward part.

Folding clothes did not always happen on laundry day at my house.

Never mistaken for twins, I did sometimes dress my boys alike. One of my favorite pictures was taken at my mom's beach house in the Outer Banks of North Carolina. The boys were on the deck and the ocean was in the background. They were wearing purple and green matching polo style L.L. Bean shirts. When the kids were still pretty young, I worked on the phones at L.L. Bean from 6 PM-midnight in the fall. We all enjoyed that discount. For some inexplicable reason, there was a dead baby shark head on the deck railing. A souvenir from a beach walk where people used big nets to fish, perhaps? Anything caught and not wanted was left on the beach to delight young boys. Of course, these treasures would need to be brought home and included in photos. Maybe that baby shark head had been named by Bobby. I can't recall, but I do know that it didn't make the long car ride back to Maine.

The boys looked healthy, tanned, and relaxed. Bobby is looking directly at the camera; his blue eyes sparkling like the ocean behind him in the afternoon sun. I imagine that he had his left arm casually draped over Jon's shoulders when the shot was set. By the time the pic had been snapped, Jon was bent sideways at the waist and trying to sneak off with Bobby's arm around his neck. Jon was also smiling, a bit impishly, at the camera. Again, this may be evidence that he understood my intentions. Perfectly.

PART 3
THE AUGHTS

It was right about when Jon turned thirteen when we moved. We moved from our seaside town (not a seaside, house to be clear) to the foothills. The schools did a great job communicating about what Jon might need in the classroom. Cape Elizabeth sent a team to Farmington to help with Jon's next transition. Our new house was an 1800 farmhouse right intown Farmington. I loved all the old details and built-ins and walking to town was fantastic. The house was constantly needing updating and was frankly, a money pit. But I loved it until after our divorce when I wanted to move back to Portland. Small town Maine had become just a bit too small for me. Sometime after we moved to Farmington, we sold the ski house. It was only about 45 minutes from the Farmington house and we weren't using it as much anymore. Dave was coaching high school basketball and Bobby had gone to UConn. Jon and I still skied, but his in-home support was set up with weekend and vacation hours and it became easier to stay home. It was also around this time that I went back to grad school for school counseling. Life was changing for us all but we did have some very special memories in all our houses.

The very first year that Jon, eight at the time, participated in Maine alpine Special Olympics (SO) at Sugarloaf he was coached by his private instructor, Mike, who was a special education student at the University of Maine at Farmington. Somehow, Jon was invited to light the torch that year. This is the torch that had been run all over Maine by law enforcement volunteers and was now his to ski to where the Olympic cauldron would be lit with the smaller torch and stay lit for the remainder of the games. It was the highlight of opening ceremonies. Mike, tall, blonde, and an all-American kid who loved skiing and Ultimate Frisbee, had a great rapport with Jon. The plan for the torch was for me to ski down a slight hill with Jon and the torch, which, of course, was on fire. Jon was small for his age and a pretty capable skier, but I was still pretty nervous about the fire part. We hiked up to where we would begin. I put him and his short skis between my longer yellow Volkl racing skis- I've never raced, but I loved those fast skis. I held the torch with one hand and put my other arm across Jon's chest, holding him close. Jon held the torch below me. Slowly, we put our skis into a wedge and headed for the podium and Mike. When we made it down the hill without harm, I somehow, handed both the torch and Jon to Mike, who then lifted Jon and guided the smaller torch to light the cauldron. The Bangor Daily News (BDN) got a great shot of the moment when Jon was transferring the flame, with Mike's help, of course. Their two faces close together. Mike was smiling with his perfectly straight teeth. Jon looked a bit confused. This was done at noon on Monday.

I tried to get a copy of that photo, but the BDN wasn't interested in selling. I was diagnosed with breast cancer about a month later at 37. I lost my drive for that project but ran into Mike years later and his dad had managed to get a copy for him. I've often regretted my quick decision to give up the photo battle.

But, back to those Special Olympic games in 2000.

Every year the S.O. winter games ran from a Sunday afternoon in January until mid-day on Tuesday. The games always begin with a welcome dinner on Sunday night and concluded with races on Tuesday. The opening ceremonies are Monday around noon. The alpine skiers were, by far, the busiest and the whole thing was exhausting and wonderful at the same time.

Alpine athletes lined up at the top of their respective courses early on Monday morning for time trials. Races were Monday afternoon and Tuesday morning. There are four courses and Jon was on the number three course. It wasn't the hardest course, but it was the only course with a cool start shack at the top.

Jon's first race was Monday afternoon after lighting the special torch. He lined up at the top with Mike. Many of the SO athletes understand the process of taking turns down the course. Jon, seemingly, did not. But there were times in upcoming years when I would swear that he DQ'd (disqualified) just because. He still doesn't like to wait. On that Monday afternoon at the end of January, temps were in the single digits and the wind was brisk. I was happy to hang down on the course a bit so I could capture his first-ever ski race on video. I had one of those big flip video cameras-not quite the boom box, 'Say Anything' scene, but you get the picture. I have no idea if it was a slalom, giant slalom or downhill course-I still don't know which is which. In any case, I skied part of the way down the course and set up next to the rope which defined the racecourse from the rest of the slope. There, I could get a video of the race. Since it was the number three course and not the uber-competitive number four course, Mike was allowed to ski in front of Jon to indicate where he should turn. Mike was instructed to stop short of the finish line so that the race time was, in fact, actually Jon's time. After that first year, I took over the role of coach and became very good at navigating the course while yelling over my shoulder, "Around the red one, around the blue one" as we turned through the gates.

But, back to that first, magical year. I posted up to shoot the video, looking uphill with the tails of my Volkl's together making a V shape to keep me from sliding back toward the lodge. I started the camera while the racers were lined up. What I remember most was watching that video at an extra fast speed. I had zoomed in on Jon and Mike and they were doing quite the dance up there as they waited for Jon's turn to slide from the shack into his first turn. I watched Jon shuffle forward and Mike shuffle with him. Then Jon would shuffle back, and Mike would follow. Lather, rinse and repeat like that old shampoo jingle from the '70s. Mike always had complete control and Jon had no chance of breaking away and heading down the slope without hitting the gates. It was hilarious to watch and something that I would learn to handle over the next ten years. I don't remember the video of Jon skiing, but it was entertaining enough to just watch him shuffle at the top.

By the time that I took over as coach in 2002 the number three course leaders were familiar with Jon and arranged heats so that he didn't have to wait long. They also often placed him in a heat of three or fewer, so he always medaled. I'm not sure that he even cared about winning a medal, but it was so very cool for me to observe. I was also able to shoot pics of him on the medal stand while one member of law enforcement presented the medal and another stood behind the medal stand and directly behind Jon to keep him from jumping off the stand onto the icy patio area, and essentially, keeping him in the frame for me. As the years went on, he became increasingly better at accepting those medals-probably so he could get off that stand more quickly.

That first year in 2000 was especially magical as it was our first and we had no idea about the diagnosis to come (for me). Life is still defined as before cancer and after cancer.

The rest of the games weren't really Jon's cup of tea. Another dinner, catered by KFC, on Monday night followed by fireworks and a dance didn't do it for Jon-especially after he adopted his gluten-free diet and had to bring his own dinner. In the early days, I was eager to go to these events, but as Jon got older, I agreed that it was better to chill at the house. Eight AM in the lodge came early on Tuesday.

~ ❖ ~

In 2000 when Jon was almost nine and Bobby newly ten, I was diagnosed with breast cancer. It's hard to describe that surreal feeling, but to say I felt knocked off my feet is probably an understatement.

I had found a lump in January. In the shower after one of my very precious workouts that began with two toddlers and free daycare for two hours and continued after the kids were in school full-time. It was something that I did for myself. I think those workouts saved me in a lot of ways. They made me stronger physically and clearer of mind.

Also, the lump discovery.

Because I was so young. I was diagnosed after surgery at a stage one, but my HER2 grade, which basically, and how I understood it, indicates how aggressive the cancer was. It was a grade 3-probably due to my 37-year-old metabolism. I caught it early and I credit that to the exercise, the after-exercise showers, and general body awareness.

And probably some luck

My PCP tried to aspirate the lump after I found it. For whatever reason, he was unable to do so. I wasn't sure if I was disappointed that he couldn't get the fluid for biopsy or if I was just happy to be done with the painful attempts. Don't get me wrong, he was a very gentle doctor-it's just that this procedure was quite painful, and the multiple attempts just made it all the worse. A mammogram was ordered. I was a full 13 years younger than the typical age for a woman to have her first mammo. It was hard to not think about what could have been had I not found that lump. These days, 21 years later, I think about it less.

I had my mammo on March 1. It was scary and it hurt. The tech was super nice and comforting and even warmed the plates before carefully placing my not-visibly lumpy right breast on the warmed plate. There was a medical center near me, so I didn't have to go into the big scary Maine Medical Center. Not yet, anyway.

Instead of having my PCP read the mammo, or perhaps after, I really can't recall, I was told to make an appointment to see a surgeon on a Monday morning in mid-March. The appointment was in a town north of Portland and my house south and east. We were skiing that weekend, so I stayed up at the mountain house on Sunday night with my neurotic Blue Tick Coon Hound, Jake, and headed out on Monday morning for my appointment. My car was running funny at speeds over 45mph, and my appointment was two hours away requiring much faster speeds than I was averaging. I called my mechanic in a panic. He quickly and effectively diagnosed that there was snow in the wheel wells from our playful run-in with a snowbank near the house the day before. We had accumulated multiple feet of snow over the season and the snowbanks made our loop of a road almost only suitable for one-way traffic. There was a curve by the house that was fun to drive around approaching from the right side. We intentionally bumped up against the bank-pretending we were surfing or something like that. It wasn't dangerous and Jon loved it. I was back on the road in minutes after using my snow brush to free the packed snow from the wheels.

The strangest, to me, part of this story is that I had my mammo film with me all weekend. This was 21 years ago when it wasn't as easy to access films from computers. In any case, I never even thought to open that large manila envelope that I protected all weekend and placed on the front seat of my green Isuzu Trooper on that cold Monday morning. If I had opened that envelope, I would have been woefully unprepared for what I saw.

At the appointment, the surgeon successfully aspirated the lump and then went to show me the film. Before I could even see it, she said, "It's time to punch a pillow." My stomach dropped. When I saw the film, I saw a lot of black with a grayish outline of my right breast. Right there, close to the surface and up toward my armpit, was a jagged orb that was blindingly white. My tumor. It looked like the most evil thing I'd ever seen. She gave me a hug and said I'd have confirmation from the aspirated fluid in a day or two.

On the 20-minute ride home I called my sister, Lee, at work in Boston. She said she'd be right up. I also called Dave at work. He was stunned. Since the kids were still at school, I was alone in the house with no idea what to do with myself. I waited for my sister to come. Lee showed up around lunchtime and we spent the afternoon looking for a distraction. Something she does very well and something I absolutely hate doing is cleaning closets. My wardrobe got a massive overhaul that afternoon. It was much needed and a worthy use of our time. At some point, Dave came home. He hadn't mentioned that he would, so I wasn't expecting him. He knew when I spoke with him that my sister was on her way. He said that he couldn't concentrate at work. Emotion was everywhere.

The next day Lee and I went to the cancer center to get some basic info. This was helpful, but also made the situation very real. When the call confirming my surgeon's suspicion came, I was prepared. I knew that I needed a team: surgeon, oncologist, and radiologist. A meeting was set up and my course of treatment was set. Surgery was scheduled for late March. The two days of waiting for my diagnosis seemed like some of the longest in my life, but once that diagnosis was made things happened with lightning speed.

My house was filled with cards and flowers-I used to say that the house smelled funereal. I still have some of the vases but donated many of them over the years. Who needs 20 vases of varying shapes and sizes? One of my favorites: clear and tall and straight (perfect for Irises who's purple, yellow, and green colors I find so pleasing), broke in my recent move. Almost 20 years later.

My dad came the day before my surgery. I had a friend at home to meet the kid's busses on surgery day as I had a late surgery-2 PM. I wasn't allowed to eat anything but was too nervous to worry much about the hunger pangs. I got to the hospital early with my dad and Dave and was whisked off to the basement nuclear medicine lab for a sentinel node biopsy. I promise you that the basement isn't the nicest part of that hospital. The plan here was to use dye and radiology to find the sentinel lymph node under my right arm. The sentinel node is the one that any cancer cells would migrate to first if they had migrated from the tumor and were catching a ride along with lymph fluid. This information allows the surgeon to remove fewer lymph nodes, allowing for better drainage and other good stuff.

In some confusion, I was late for that appointment. I'm not really sure where the confusion came from, but I know that they were worried that they wouldn't get the x-ray info in time and surgery would have to be postponed. I was not having that happen (again, my type-A personality showing through).

I was lying on the table under the x-ray machine in the hospital basement after the dye had been inserted into my tumor. The same tumor that I just had to have taken out of my body. It drove me crazy to know that I had a tumor in me for those few weeks between diagnosis and surgery. I asked the x-ray tech how long these procedures usually took. Her vague answer was that it was different for everyone and could take up to a couple of hours. By my calculation, I had about 30 minutes before I would lose my surgery spot. I was under that machine with my eyes closed. She took an x-ray every two minutes to gauge the progress. Nothing was happening. When I started picturing my thumbs pushing the lymph fluid toward the node-she began to see progress. My imagery was working. She pinned the spot on the final x-ray, and I was able to proceed to surgery. Many years later I had a friend tell me that if you wanted to get something done, "Just ask Ellie."

She was talking about high school football fundraisers.

I woke from surgery feeling very nauseated. This is typical for me as I remember many baby tooth extractions done in my childhood under full anesthesia. The nurse told me to take an anti-nausea pill and sleep for two hours. At 7 PM they asked me to leave as I was only in for day surgery. I had a hard time sitting up and getting dressed, but I finally made my way to Dave's car. It was a miserable ride home with a stop at the pharmacy so I could take the meds. I was helped to bed and woke, in two hours, feeling much better. A couple of days later I received the report that margins and lymph nodes were clean.

Good news, indeed!

At the time I had 40 hours of in-home support each week for Jon after school. This was the maximum amount allowed with funding and essential in having the time I needed to recover from surgery while preparing for chemotherapy.

Two days after surgery, my neighbor, a nurse, came to my house to tape up my drain so that I could shower. How I hated that damn drain. It was in the way, and it pulled on my skin if I moved the wrong way or too quickly. I also hated draining the damn drain-always afraid that I would do something wrong. The damn drain was a long flexible tube that was surgically placed under my right arm where seven lymph nodes had been removed at the same time as the tumor in my breast. The flexible tube was close to my body, but placed, by me when dressing, between the tank top (no bras until after radiation) and my shirt. It had a bulb at the end which collected the fluid. On top of the bulb was a plug to keep the fluid in until I was ready to empty it, usually a couple of times a day. I had to wear it pinned to my shirt on the outside. I looked like a sick person with that damn drain. I went to my surgeon for a checkup and asked (demanded, really, but in a nice way) that she take out the damn drain. She didn't want to because I wasn't healed enough, but I was pretty persistent-a skill that had served me well bullying school officials and others into necessary services for Jon. She removed the damn drain and I had to see her two more times for her to aspirate a lump of lymph fluid that sat under the skin of my underarm, the size of an egg, with no damn drain to let it escape. The third time, I didn't get to her in time and the egg-sized sac of fluid just burst all over me. I was taking a break from my part-time job at a private library, sitting at a pool watching Jon swim in the local Special Olympics and I remember I was wearing a white tank (remember, no bras until treatment was over) and a white shirt. I've never participated in a wet tee-shirt contest, but I think that was pretty close. I hustled home to change and went back to my part-time job. Humiliated, but clean and dry.

A woman from town who volunteered to swim with Jon weekly was in the pool with him encouraging him to swim across in the lane. He was perfectly capable of this, but he stopped halfway across. He liked being in the pool. Why would he swim to the other side and have to get out? I can only assume that was what he was thinking.

Jon did not medal that day.

I skied about ten days after my surgery. I was still very tender and skied without poles and with my right arm protecting my chest. I imagined that I looked a bit like a clipped bird in my yellow parka and yellow skis one arm swopping through turns and the other held tightly to my body.

Chemo was set to begin in April. I chose the most aggressive combo of drugs that was offered-mostly because of my age and otherwise relatively good health. I delayed the first treatment until after April break because I wasn't sure how I would feel, and I didn't want my kids to see me sick. Plus, I had to take care of them during school break.

I cut my long hair in preparation for its eventual loss.

Twice.

I had worn my hair long. Not long like in high school where I sported the parted in the middle and stick straight Marcia Brady (think Brady Bunch) look as best I could with my wavy brown locks. My hair was probably my biggest vanity for most of my life to this point. The thought of losing it was disheartening.

The irony was/is not lost on me.

I had four chemo treatments that were three weeks apart. I needed a driver for these visits. Dave took a turn or two and my mom came up from Virginia for one. I think a friend or two also came with me. The routine was to check in, have bloodwork done for white counts and such, and then move to the treatment room where I sat in a recliner and hooked up to an IV drip. I have always had this thing about reclining chairs. I didn't like them before chemo, and I really object to them now. Being force-fed poison in one did nothing for my loathing of the symbol of American's need for ultimate comfort. I didn't have a port surgically inserted into my chest, so I just provided the best vein in my left arm. I could feel the chemo (poison) in my nose-it tingled if the drip was too fast and drove me a little nuts-to this day I can recall that awful sensation just by thinking about it-like right now. I also became sleepy-thus the driver. After about an hour the bag was fully emptied, and I was free to go home and sleep away the afternoon.

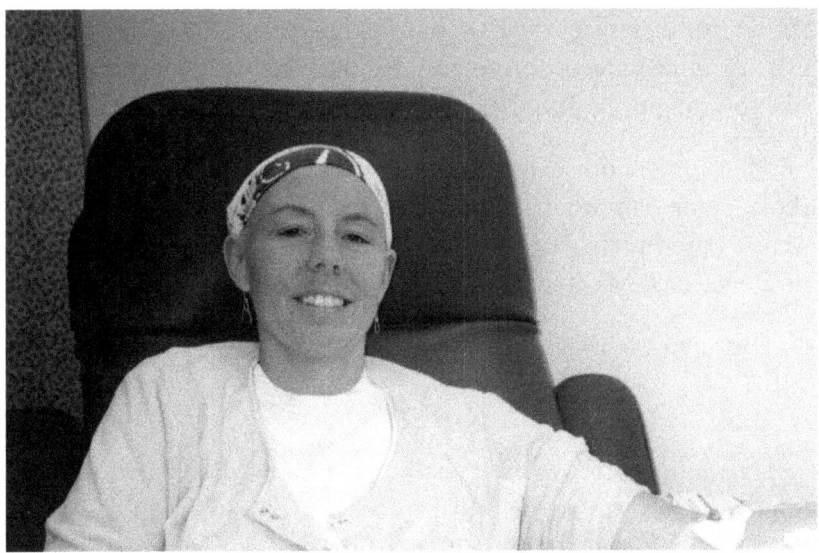

The first chemo contained Prednisone and it made me crazy. I couldn't sleep at night and my mind raced. My oncologist adjusted that in later chemo treatments. The anti-nausea pills were huge and made me miserably constipated. I was tired and felt sick, so I didn't work for a few days after each treatment. I developed mouth sores after three of the four treatments. Those blister-like things on the roof and sides of my mouth and tongue made it almost impossible to eat. They were essentially like big canker sores. Especially at the tip of, and under my tongue. The gross lidocaine mouthwash didn't really help. I missed drinking wine at night. At my first chemo treatment, a friend who was also going through chemo brought me a pink rose. Chemo still sucked.

After my first chemo treatment, my workmates came with me to a barber where I had my now bobbed hair, cut, yet again to about an inch long all over, and then my head shaved. Pictures were taken and ice cream was consumed. I timed the appointment for ten days after the treatment because I was told that my hair would start falling out around 12 days after treatment. I knew that I couldn't bear having it all come out in clumps in the shower. So much for not looking sick. I wore bandanas on my head to keep warm. I was ridiculously cold the entire time I was going through chemo and the air conditioning in the grocery store would make my eyes and nose run like faucets. Jon refused to touch my bald head. He didn't like to look at me. It broke my heart.

When my mom came to town, we went hat shopping. I wore those fancy hats when I was working in the Old Port or when we went out to lunch. The pictures of the models for the hat shop ads in Down East Magazine looked great in the hats.

They had eyebrows and eyelashes.

During this time many people made many, many meals for the family, which was so helpful because I had zero interest in food. People also knew how much time Jon and I spent together and wanted to help with that. Being non-verbal, and really sloppy at traditional American Sign Language (ASL) proved to be a barrier, but not one that couldn't be overcome. The elementary school social worker and the school speech therapist actually held a few sessions with interested people on how to best communicate with

Jon should they chose to venture out with him alone. After these sessions, my friends felt comfortable enough to pick Jon up and take him to a playground or beach for a much-appreciated hour of respite for me.

At that time, I had a part-time job abstracting articles in a private library. It wasn't a huge staff, but I had two colleagues who were still in their 20's. They were the ones eating ice cream with me when I had my head shaved. They were single and not long out of college. I don't think that they attended one of Pam and Suzie's sessions, but they did offer to take Jon to McDonald's for lunch one day.

After about an hour, I began to wonder about the lunching trio, but cell phones weren't what they are today. I can't remember, but I probably just changed the CD and returned to the couch that seemed to be my home base when someone else was watching Jon and while I was undergoing chemo and later radiation.

When they finally returned Jon, after about 90 minutes, and with at least three hours worth of stories, I got the lowdown. He got his usual happy meal and didn't steal French fries from any other customers. So far so good.

After eating, he then climbed to the top of the slide. He wouldn't come down. It was lunchtime and there were other playland loving tots-most much younger than nine-year-old Jon. My co-workers were desperate to unclog the situation but to no avail. He wasn't budging. He didn't appear to be upset or scared. He appeared to be watching the growing activity around him with great interest.

The shorter of the two women, (these things aren't built for adults, so size is relative) tried to climb in and join Jon at the top of the slide and coax him down. I don't recall the details, (chemo brain is real), but it might have been an ice cream cone that finally did the trick-and got that child down the slide opening it up for the so many others who were patiently waiting.

Upon returning, and after the approximately three hours of stories, they offered continued help-anything except taking Jon.

I'm happy to say that this experience didn't scare them away from becoming moms-just not right after that lunch.

Another chemo-based Jon story included a friend of mine who has three kids of her own. Because she is a good person, she was happy to take Jon for a few hours to give me a break. She did attend one of the communication sessions. She also organized many, many meals for my family during the chemo and radiation process. I think the meal part is more in her wheelhouse, but God love her, she took Jon for an afternoon. The plan was to take Jon to McDonald's (for the playland and French fries, of course) and after that, a trip to the local playground.

Armed with a bag of gummy bears (because this was how Jon's behavior was and still is modified), and her tween-aged daughter, my friend showed up to take Jon out. They headed out towards the mall; a good fifteen-minute ride-to find the McDonald's with the best playland. Jon and my friend's daughter were sitting in the back seat during the ride. Apparently, the gummies didn't last the ride to the restaurant. The bag should have lasted the day or several, but desperate times and tween co-pilots will sometimes mess with the gummy to behavior ratio. Also, Jon can be very charming when he wants gummies.

In any case, they arrived at McDonald's and had their meal and play time. Jon was happy and they soon departed for a playground in Cape Elizabeth. This was when they realized that the magic to the outing was with the gummies, so they stopped at a Dollar store for an emergency stash for the fifteen-minute ride to the playground. Jon was returned to me happy and maybe a bit high on sugar, but none the worse for the wear.

Again, this was a one-time outing. I really believe that the thought of being in charge of Jon is more daunting than the actual being in charge of Jon, but after several people took him out once and decided that they could help in other ways, I have to think that being with Jon can be stressful.

Good to know that my feelings have been validated.

I had little appetite for food, especially for the five days after each chemo treatment. We were going to put Jon on a gluten-free diet to see if that would help with his speech but decided to delay that for a year until I had more energy and control over what he ate as many meals were delivered and gratefully accepted. Dave's company provided meals every single Monday for six months. Someone had or bought a basket, and every department would take turns filling this basket that Dave would bring home every Monday. It always had a complete meal and there was always enough food for two nights. I didn't even lose one pound during my chemo time. I hadn't had a glass of wine in months and virtually skipped four days of meals every three weeks. When I mentioned this to my doctor, she replied that most people gained weight during chemo.

I stopped complaining.

The gluten-free diet started a year later. No speech was recovered, but it is still helpful with his behaviors. I only allowed myself to wonder if I had squandered that year and if we might have had a better result had we changed his diet the year we planned to a few times. It's so hard to not think in terms of what if.

It's also really not helpful in the long run.

I had a month between chemo and radiation, and I tried to be as active as possible. I had missed that part of my life with chemo draining every ounce of non-essential energy from my body. I did manage to keep my part-time job and only missed a few days after each treatment. I also had a work-at-home option for days that I just wasn't up for driving into the office. We were so far ahead of the world on this one! One week in July we went to Sugarloaf and put the kids in day camp. I biked, hiked, got lost hiking and biking, and wore myself out, but in a good way.

One of the things that bothered me most during chemo was being forced into a temporary four-month menopause. Plenty of time for that experience later! Another thing that really bugged me was my lack of attention to reading. My job was writing abstracts on corporate governance in a private library and I think that took all I had. I barely had the energy to read a magazine article back then. Maybe that's why I still start reading magazine articles and rarely finish them today. As I mentioned, chemo brain is real. I didn't read many books during that time and the few that I did read I remember absolutely nothing about. I really should reread The Pilots Wife.

I hear that it's excellent.

Radiation fatigue is supposed to be cumulative. I had 33 treatments over the course of six and a half weeks. I was napping on the couch after the very first treatment. Radiation kicked my ass.

I had a radiation routine. I would rollerblade down a big hill near the grange in Cape Elizabeth every morning. I rollerbladed back up that hill as well. After my exercise, I would shower and head to treatment. My treatments were 30 minutes from door to door. Before I started treatment, I went in to have a mold made that would pinpoint where the radiation needed to go (over the scar on my right breast). With this mold came permanent marks on my chest. My tattoos. Now they look like freckles, but they were important in guiding my treatment. I'm glad that my doctor used brown ink-I've heard of some women who were marked with blue.

Once in my gown and in the treatment room, I would be placed on a table and the mold/shield would be placed correctly for the radiation to begin. I don't know how long it took-a minute? Five? It didn't hurt and I didn't burn as some patients do, but man was I tired. I had to take a leave from my job because I just couldn't drag myself to work or even work from home. Other than my workouts

I spent most of my days sleeping until the kids got off their busses. This fatigue carried past the end of the treatment-for weeks.

One day when I was feeling better, Bobby got off his bus and let himself into the house to see me standing up. He, very eloquently, pointed out that I wasn't asleep on the couch. He always came home first because Jon began riding the special bus (I really object to the term short bus and I'm still not sure that special is a whole lot better) with a one-on-one aide after some antics on the regular bus. Bobby's appearance always let me know that it was time to pull myself together to get Jon in the house and feed him a snack before his in-home support person came to start his or her shift.

By fall, my hair was coming in. I was lucky, I didn't have the downy peach fuzz type of hair that some cancer patients have in the beginning. Mine came in dark and straight like a crew cut. There are many pictures of me holding Jon that fall. It was easier to hold him than to chase him. I remember one picture in particular where we were watching Bobby play football. It was around my September birthday and there was a huge birthday cake. I was the president of Cape Elizabeth Youth Football at the time. I had nine-year-old Jon on my hip to prevent him from running away, our backs to the camera. I was wearing a long-sleeved shirt and a fleece vest and sunglasses. It was a glorious day. Small, padded boys in helmets were running around on the field. Those football players thought my crew cut was so cool!

Eventually, the crew cut became an unruly mass of chemo curls. I had ringlets. I had no idea what to do with all these curls-neither did the hairdresser in Virginia who tried to tame them for my brother's wedding the following April. I had a legit afro during that very windy outdoor wedding. I was no longer aspiring to have Marcia Brady hair.

When Jon was ten, he had a lot of energy. A lot! He also had an in-home support person who had a lot of energy; a lovely man going to grad school and working with us on the side. This was a fabulous combination. No couch potatoes here. Jon and his in-home-support person did all sorts of things together. They played soccer for a Special Olympic team, which meant that Jon mostly ran around the field. One lovely summer day I took Jon and, Wrigley the Newf, on one of the Casco Bay ferries to Great Diamond Island where Jon's person was house-sitting for some friends. He picked us up at the ferry terminal in a golf cart and brought us to the most beautiful compound that I've ever seen. I was terrified. I didn't want Jon inside even for a minute, which was fine because the plan was for the boys to Kayak around the island while the girls, Wrigley and me, sat on the deck and sunned ourselves silly. Jon's guy did all the kayaking and Jon sat in front, probably directing his caregiver. After an outside lunch we, (Jon, Wrig., and I) headed back to reality.

The thing that they did most often didn't include cars, boats, or golf carts. They loved to go rollerblading on a local greenbelt trail. They would skate for miles through the park and down to the other park with a lighthouse on the bay. The only problem with this activity, for Jon at least, was the requirement (mine) that Jon wear a helmet. It was purple and he wore the chin strap loose (my compromise). It was a struggle to get him to put in on, but he liked the rollerblading enough to comply. Until the day he didn't.

Jon didn't just refuse to wear the helmet. In fact, he started out wearing it. All was going well until they crossed a cement bridge that crossed a small creek. Jon's support person stopped when Jon stopped, but not in time to save the purple helmet from getting tossed into the creek where it quickly floated away-never to be seen again.

Bolting, for Jon, started almost before he could walk and lasted for many years.

Bolting was never limited to open water. A slightly older (ten) Jon was roaming around our ski house during a party. He still had a few months before starting a gluten-free diet so I wasn't as vigilant about keeping an eye on him with the food situation because stealing food wasn't yet on my radar, as it would become in the next couple of years and to this day.

There were lots of adults and a bunch of kids in attendance. The fridge was full, and the beer was out in the snow on the deck. It was Christmas week and very cold outside. Like single digits cold.

Fahrenheit.

Because it's hard, (impossible), to turn down a woodstove once it's been fully stoked and filled, we had a window without a screen partially open to the deck. The deck lights were on and festive Christmas lights allowed people to see all the snow that had yet to be shoveled off the deck. The very snow that was keeping beer icy cold.

Sugarloaf was, at the time, considered Portland North. I think it still is today. In any case, lots of our friends from the Portland area had places up there or were visiting for the Christmas week. We often had friends staying with us.

It was in this snow that a tall friend spotted Jon. No one saw Jon climb out the screenless window from the black leather couch that sat beneath it, but his tiny leg prints in the snow led us to believe that this is exactly what happened. Our tall friend saw him first and charged out the French door. He returned, carried a crying, and very pissed off, Jon over his shoulder and back into the house. Our tall friend was over his knees in the snow that had yet to be shoveled. Imagine what tiny Jon could do with all that snow.

My brother was married in April of 2001. I mention this because it was a great opportunity for a week-long party. I flew to Virginia with Jon and one of his teachers who was accompanying us to help look after Jon during our family time. As Jon's special education teacher, she knew Jon well. She knew what he was capable of and what he might get into. Dave and Bobby came down a day or two later.

My mom and stepdad's house was set on a little peninsula that jutted into a river in Virginia. At the end of the peninsula was a fishing pier with a boat and some oyster traps that my stepdad had set up. This was our home base during that wedding week. Thursday night my mother and stepdad had a party at the house for all out-of-town guests. It was a beautiful night and about 30 people came by for a catered BBQ-not burgers and dogs, but real Southern BBQ. The house was opened up and the breeze blew spring air through the open windows. There was a tent with a DJ on the lawn between the house and the pier. Sometime before dinner Jon got away from all watching eyes and made his way out to the pier. As quick as he was, he was in the water before anyone could stop him. I think he broke one of the oyster traps with his fall. I don't really know how he didn't get hurt. We fished him out and his teacher took him inside to shower and change for dinner. Jon and his teacher came back outside to join the party and have some food. I remember listening to Dave Matthews from the speakers while sipping wine with my sister and my bourbon drinking brother and his wife-to-be. It was all very civilized, and dinner was yummy. The warm Virginia sun felt wonderful on my face after another long Maine winter.

Shortly after dinner, I checked on the kids. Bobby was bored. He was 12 at an adult party. I get it. I found Jon in the kitchen with his teacher and some other people. He seemed to be doing well. I went back out to mingle. Back out to the tent. As the sun was beginning to set, I heard a bit of a commotion. All eyes were on Jon walking out of the river on the side of the house. He had entered it through a stand of trees that blocked the view of the closest neighbor. I didn't see him enter, but I did catch him, on film, walking out. He was wearing an orange short-sleeved button shirt. It was a pretty shade of orange-almost more salmon and looked great with his dark hair which was completely soaked. The shirt was clinging to him and had several buttons undone. Jon's pants were dark from the water. His grin was huge. He was very proud of himself. His teacher met Jon where the trees met the grass and hauled him back into the house to shower and change, yet again. There was no point yelling at Jon-that was never a thing because loud noises made him very upset. There wasn't even a consequence because, really, what could I do? He knew that I wasn't happy with him, but he didn't care or couldn't help himself.

Later that night Jon went to bed before the rest of us. It was a huge house but only had three bedrooms so our family of four was sharing a room with an ensuite bath. The accommodations were lovely but tight. He was restless that night and couldn't settle down. This was before he was medicated for sleep. We couldn't really hear him because the party had moved inside, and somehow, the lovely four-poster bed became a three-poster bed that night. It's a family joke now, but I can assure you that my stepfather was never amused. Jon never did return to that house. Again, we had no idea what happened, but he definitely broke that bed.

The rest of the weekend was uneventful, at least as far as Jon was concerned. Friday night was the rehearsal dinner at the country club. Jon and his teacher stayed in a hotel near Williamsburg where the outdoor wedding would be held at a nearby antebellum mansion. We explored Williamsburg and enjoyed the wedding on Saturday. On Sunday all the guests scattered to our respective homes.

Before the wedding, there was a lot of talk about whether Jon should come with us to Virginia. We knew he wouldn't attend the ceremony or reception, but I was pretty insistent that he be part of the family to his best ability. In retrospect, he probably didn't need to leave Maine. He did enjoy himself-even outside of the river so that helped. Now, I don't take him too far from his group home. He is more comfortable there and it's best for everyone in my changed opinion.

Clearly, Jon had ideas about where he wanted or needed to be, and he was very good at sneaking out of our eyesight. It would seem that he wasn't being looked after, but I assure you, he was just of single mind and purpose and not to be denied.

Autism is a condition where communication as most people know it is compromised. Some people are better at it than others. Jon, as I've mentioned, is almost completely, non-verbal. He uses a few sloppy signs that barely resemble the American Sign Language (ASL) signs that we all learned when he was very young. He still signs friendship when he is told to wait because his ed-tech in first grade had him wait with his hands in his lap and intertwining his fingers. This looks like the sign for friendship (more or less). He has also used the Picture Exchange Communication System (PECS), which can be used on a big white communication board. There are Velcro strips on the board which are designed to hold small pictures of objects, emotions, wants and needs like food or drink. Jon could go to his board and choose a want (like ice cream). He could then present this one-inch square laminated card with a picture of ice cream on the front and Velcro on the back to whoever might be able to get that ice cream for him. We had hundreds of words to use on that board and even made the house a virtual board by Velcro-ing items to the walls. There was a bathroom card outside the bathroom. He would present this card when he wanted to use the bathroom. It was a way to increase his vocabulary and he learned the meaning of a lot of words. He says none of them clearly.

We went through rolls of Velcro!

Much later Jon was identified as a 'very lazy communicator' as the result of a speech evaluation. He had Proloqu2go on a very antiquated iPad that is really just PECS in a digital and much less cumbersome format. He still really only uses his iPad to ask for ice cream and to go for a ride. Occasionally, if he's feeling really cheeky, he will combine the two and ask to go for a ride to get ice cream. The first time he did this I was delighted. He was getting the communication thing.

He was so proud of himself and probably thought he was so clever. He often slammed the iPad shut with the great expectation of mint chocolate chip. Now, I'm over it, and he can't be getting ice cream multiple times a day. The ice cream has been removed from the iPad.

But, again, I digress.

It's my theory that when he was younger, he had times when he was less than interested in attending school every day. This is a theory because he couldn't tell me when he wasn't feeling the school thing. He may be non-verbal, but he is clever and has ways of getting his needs met.

It was fourth grade when Jon had trouble staying in school. Behavior was well managed by his teacher and ed-tech so tantrums and acting out didn't get the desired result of me coming to pick him up from school allowing him to come home and hang out.

Somehow, he discovered that if he poked his ear repeatedly then he would, at the very least, get a walk to see the school nurse. If he made his ear red enough and acted like it was very painful, (read: act cranky), he could sometimes convince the school nurse that he had an ear infection. They are very painful, as I can recall from my own childhood, so, of course, the school nurse was paying attention and would attempt to console Jon. While Jon could be consoled, he would not, however, let her use an otoscope to confirm redness, and perhaps, fluid, in his ear.

The school nurse called home and I called the doctor before picking him up. After this happened a couple of times, and after taking Jon to see the doctor the very afternoon that he was trying to ditch school, I realized that I was being played. Not by the school nurse: she was being played, too.

This is the same child who figured out exactly where and how to squeeze my kneecap to make me scream. I would swear, and drop his hand, which freed him to run away from me.

My best guess is that he used his body to figure out how this move, and others, would work when applied to a situation that he'd rather not be in. What works to get out of school and what works to get away from mom. These were his objectives.

Communication, in its least complicated form, is touch. Jon knows this.

Back in 2001 and sometime during the summer, a trip to Disney was planned. It was a year after I finished breast cancer treatment. It also happened to be scheduled for six weeks after 9/11.

The significance of 9/11, other than being a turning point for our country, had more to do with a gloriously empty theme park and equally empty planes. We didn't plan this, of course, but it certainly worked in our favor. The empty park part-not the terrorism part.

We woke the kids, (aged 10 and 11), early and surprised them with plane tickets with Mickey Mouse ears on the cover. Jon, a fan of exactly three Disney movies, wasn't exactly pleased but was willing to go on an adventure. His brother scowled at the early hour. We were off to a great start!

With a handicapped park pass in hand, we spent our first day at the park cycling around the line at the Aladdin ride. This is one of his three favorite movies, and the ride involves water. Win, win. The handicapped pass allowed our family to cut lines. The lines weren't bad because the traveling public was not traveling, but still, we could do that ride several times in an hour. Fun.

Our early November visit was eerily impacted by the recent September events. Corporate travel was still, largely, suspended, at least up and down the east coast, and the baseball world series was still being played. In November. Baseball in October had temporarily, lost its meaning. It was a "baseball in November" kind of year. Also, as mentioned earlier, the park was pretty empty of tourists. I began to see the magic in the Kingdom!

The lack of business travel made for relatively empty planes and terminals, which is always a good thing when traveling with a highly sensitive ten-year-old with autism. Less hustle and bustle and more peace. Since we were already traveling, Dave stayed down in Florida for work and I sat in the very last row of the plane with the kids on the way home. I had Bobby block, Jon, in the row when I needed to use the restroom-no lines. Easy peasy.

The World Series ended a seven-game series on November 4th. Jon's brother and dad watched the Arizona Diamondbacks beat the New York Yankees at a poolside bar. Those two Red Sox fans were quite happy with the result. Jon, already having put his pool time in, was in the hotel room with me. We were getting our beauty sleep to be fresh for our pre-arranged photo in the morning with the cast of Beauty and the Beast, another of his three favorite Disney movies. I wanted to read for a bit, but Jon was in a 'lights out' mood that night.

This was way before Kindles.

The following day dawned bright and sunny and our little family hopped on the mostly empty Disney bus to begin our adventure. I don't recall the exact events, but I'm sure that Jon and I were back on the Aladdin ride in the morning.

The Beauty and the Beast production was amazing, and the cast met with us for a family photo and a photo with just Jon. Sadly, my camera was broken, but Belle and Gaston offered to meet with us later in the day. I purchased a disposable camera. Memories were made. That photo is in Jon's bedroom in his group home.

I look exhausted in the family photo.

It was a long day and plans were made to meet at 5 PM at the information center to make dinner plans. Jon and I waited, patiently, for the others, who took the opportunity to explore Space Mountain. Being before cell phones that weren't in huge bags and in cars, we had no way of knowing that Space Mountain had been temporarily shut down. Half the family, having spent a good chunk of time in line, chose to wait it out.

The tardiness at our meeting point caused a phenomenon, which is known today as 'hangry'. Jon was both hungry and angry and there wasn't much that I could do about it if we were still to meet the Space Mountain crew. Sadly, I had no emergency snacks on hand that day.

A well-meaning Dwarf approached us to see if he/she could be of some assistance. Snow White is *not* one of Jon's three favorite Disney movies-101 Dalmations, in case you were curious, is the third. In any case, ten-year-old Jon, was not in the mood to be soothed and he quickly, and before I had any time to prepare, bopped the dwarf on the nose. The quick motion surprised all but Jon and we quickly moved our waiting spot to the front steps. No harm (I hope), those faces look like they have a lot of padding. Hangry Jon is still a force to be reckoned with, but he can mostly keep his hands to himself.

Skiing came into Jon's life at just the right time. He was struggling with some impulsive behaviors (bolting!), he could be highly irritable and had trouble expressing himself. For safety's sake, I had to insist that Jon stay by my side when bolting might occur. No running into traffic on my watch. Once introduced to skiing, Jon took to it like a fish to water. It was calming and met his sensory needs at the time. He could experience freedom and cruised the trails at Sugarloaf with confidence and the freedom of not being attached to another human. It also met the needs of our family. It was, literally, the only thing that we could do together. As a family.

Pretty powerful stuff and we jumped in with both feet-feeding our separate and collective needs.

We, Jon and me especially, spent countless days and nights at our ski place in western Maine. We skied the expert terrain black diamonds and in a few cases, the super steep double blacks. We skied the bumps-mostly Jon, but I did when I had to. We skied the woods-he loved it and I swore a lot as trees tried to trip me up in my quest to keep Jon in my sights. We did puzzles, jumped on huge trampolines that were brought to the anti-gravity center for training future US Ski and Snowboard Olympians, soaked in hot tubs at the club, and had lots of spontaneous fun while at our special happy place.

Currently, Jon is not considering himself a skier. This makes me so very sad. It was so good for him, but I saw him struggle with the scraping noises from other skiers and snowboarders that made him jump when they came too close to him. I really think that he is over skiing. I've tried to get him to re-engage, but last year when I pulled his ski boots from the closet and he immediately put them back in, I knew that I was in for a battle if I pushed the ski thing. Communication.

Well played, Jon. Well played.

Skiing for Jon was therapeutic. Skiing with Jon was tough. Not so much when he was just learning. That was fine. I became good at the harness and controlling his speed with the ropes. The harness was a contraption that went around his chest and abdomen and had two long straps that I held in my hands to keep him from bolting. Like the reins on a horse, I could attempt to try to initiate turns with the reins/straps. I was in a constant snowplow form, which was ski tips together and tails wide with very bent knees. I can tell you that it's so much easier to swoop parallel turns than it is to sustain a snowplow at agonizingly slow speeds. When he began to hone his skills things changed. It was still good for him, but more challenging for me as he became more adept.

Jon started out with private lessons because a bolter in sneakers is still a bolter on skis-and much harder to contain without one-one supervision. These lessons were only a couple of hours a day and expensive, but Jon had some really great one-one instructors. One year he had a nurse from Australia who was spending her summer, our winter, on leave and teaching skiing at Sugarloaf. She was fantastic and introduced me to the concept of muscle memory. Jon was currently skiing with a harness and not really getting the concept of the wedge turn. Really, he wasn't feeling turning at all. She told me to put his ski boots on every night and sit him on the edge of the bed. She then said to take a ski boot in each hand and turn the toes in and heels out. And, to do this 200 times per night. I happily packed up his ski boots for the week at home so that we could practice our new routine. I did this for a week and that next Saturday he was getting the wedge at Sugarloaf. His instructor knew what she was talking about and those two would ride the Moose Caboose, basically a snowmobile with a big sled for kids to sit on while they go up the bunny slope to practice these new turns!

It was a couple of years in when I discovered Maine Handicapped Skiing (MHS). They were a Godsend! MHS took Jon for several ski days per season. I dropped him off at 9, met him for lunch at noon, and returned him to MHS to ski from 1-3 PM.

This time with dedicated volunteers helped Jon to increase his skills, (maybe too much), and allowed me to ski without purposefully going into the trees or over the moguls-Jon's favorite terrain.

Jon's trail choices provide proprioceptive input by compressing his hip and knee joints. It was calming for him and challenging for me. I never venture into the woods or onto the moguls willingly these days.

Jon started out at MHS with a one-one skier. It wasn't long before he needed a two-one ratio, simply because he had a tendency to take off. There was even that one day where he was paired with three adults, and one of those adults was his occupational therapist from school and an excellent skier. He ditched them momentarily but was captured before he made it to the lift.

Jon is very good with navigation and skiing was no different than driving in the car. In fact, Jon modified my driving behavior because I couldn't drive by a McDonald's, like on the way to Sugarloaf, without hearing the wrath of Jon from the back seat. He can't speak, but he makes his needs known, and back in those days he felt like he needed McDonald's French fries or a Happy Meal every time we passed those glowing arches. I know this because he would flap his arms and legs in his passenger-side rear car seat and make desperate and incredibly high-pitched noises. Back to the mountain. He knew Sugarloaf Mountain like the back of his hand. Every trail, every perceived trail, every woodsy cut-through-you get the picture.

Jon was pretty good for the volunteers at MHS at the beginning; before he started pulling shenanigans. This is more about the shenanigans than his good behavior. One thing he did just a couple of times was to release his ski while on the chairlift. Who does that? It was never in a place where people could ski below and I'd like to think his choice of dumping area was intentional and with safety in mind, but still.

The first time that he did this, MHS called ski patrol and he was transported from the tippy-top of the mountain to his 'lost' ski, by toboggan. Turned out, he liked a good toboggan ride, guided and managed by ski patrol. This, clearly, wasn't the way to manage such a behavior, but I loved MHS for trying.

The next time he dropped a ski from the chair he was made to ski down on one ski. No problem for Jon, but also not as rewarding as the ski patrol guided sled ride. Still, he persisted. At least one more time. I knew that I had to come up with a solution so that I didn't lose MHS.

I started skiing in the '70s. Equipment was different back then, and as luck would have it, I still had a very special pair of Hexcel skis. The very same skis that were featured on a Hexcel ad that was shot on the Carrabassett River in the '70s. That was five years before I even knew that Sugarloaf Mountain existed. I mention this because if necessity is the mother of invention, as the anonymous Latin saying would have us believe, and you may see where this is going, those old Hexcel's came in very handy.

I removed the old, cracked leather, safety straps and figured out how to attach them to Jon's bindings. This system worked, in a sense, but it made getting Jon ready to ski immensely harder. Getting those straps around his ankles was impossible with gloves on. I braced myself around his body, got the strap with the solid end into the strap with the circle on the end, and held him in place while getting my gloves back on and jumping into my own skis. It's very cold at Sugarloaf-my hands were always cold-this didn't help.

This solution did not stop the behavior, but it decidedly created a safer atmosphere for other skiers. Occasionally, Jon still released a ski while on the chair. I might catch his falling, yet still attached, ski with one of mine. If I was lucky and caught the ski, I then proceeded to pull multiple muscles trying to get it back, at least, to the footrest of the safety bar. Often, if I wasn't paying attention, his ski would dangle straight down, but still attached to his leg by those leather safety straps. Regardless, the chair had to stop at the top for Jon to get off with one ski on and the other dragging. Very occasionally, I was successful at getting the ski back on his boot before the top of the mountain.

What did I learn from this? It's really hard to stay one step ahead of this kid!

Eventually, Jon tired of this game. Thank goodness.

One thing that seems to be consistent with people with autism is their love for water. I can't speak for all, but this has certainly proven to be true with Jon.

Many times, I would find myself taking him up to the ski house by myself or with his brother. Every Friday night. All the long Maine winter. Rather than try to plan to cook once we arrived in a cold and dark house I would often stop for pizza on the way. There was a specific place, which was about 3 miles from the house and the pizza was awesome. They had a game room in the basement. I'm not sure if it's still there, but it was good entertainment for Bobby, who could go down there by himself to see what was up. Jon would hang out with me unless I could bribe his brother to take him downstairs for a bit.

The bar area of the restaurant was always packed on Friday night. Locals who had been skiing during the day or just locals who wanted a night out joined the hordes of condo and homeowners who flocked to the mountain every Friday night from Thanksgiving until mid-April. We were that last group.

The weekend and school vacation people.

Every Friday night I would hope to score at least one seat at the bar on the way to our house. It was over two hours to the restaurant so if I timed it right, I could get there when happy hour was ending and the locals would leave-opening up a space or two for us. I would order a pizza and a glass of wine while I waited for the pizza to cook. It sounds perfectly relaxing, right? As a part-time worker and mostly stay-at-home mom, I was hungry for adult conversation, whether I was actually participating or just watching with a glass of Sonoma-Cutrer Chardonnay. This was a special time in my week.

The place was always hustling and when Jon joined me at the bar with his unending glass of ginger ale it was always exciting. Jon was happy to have his drink, but eventually, he would crave water and, not the kind you drink. He wasn't thirsty. This could go two ways. He could ask to go to the men's room and play in the sink, where I would hope that his brother was available to accompany him or it could be a decidedly less appealing option.

There were times when Jon, who was just a tiny thing, back in the day, would try to get behind the bar. This could be a duck and run operation, where he would, literally, duck under the small opening and run to the sink where the bar-backing magic happened. If he didn't employ the duck and run, he was equally capable of getting himself onto the bar top and over onto the other side in the blink of an eye. I could be sitting at a stool with my leg wrapped protectively around him one minute and watching him playing in the sink on the other side of the massive wood bar the next. I can't tell you how many times he was handed back over the bar to me. And I really was paying attention. He was just that crafty and fast!

This wasn't the only bar where Jon voluntarily tried to bar back, essentially playing with water while glasses are being rinsed in the sink. Another bar at Sugarloaf was a favorite Après place back in those early days. Often, I would take Jon by myself-the other males busy with basketball. He was, in no way, the only kid in the bar. He was, most likely, the most active. Always searching for a way to get over or around that large slab of oak that separated him from his beloved water.

I distinctly remember one night when a friend from Cape Elizabeth was sitting at the bar. His wife on one side and little Jonny on the other. I was on the other side of Jon attempting to communicate with adults while keeping order-or simply keeping Jon on my side, (the customer side) of the bar.

Jon being Jon was faster. Also, let's face it, Ginger Ale is decidedly better than Chardonnay in situations that require quickness and agility after a day on the slopes. Unless it's the fifth Chardonnay-then you are a rock star who can do anything.

I was not on my fifth Chard and Jon did attempt a vault over the bar. My friend was somehow able to grab his tiny waist just before his short legs flipped over with the expectation of hitting the ground and heading for the sink. Jon tried, somehow, to get out of the very shirt that I was holding. This left me holding a shirt and shirtless Jon was free to jump the bar.

This same friend, who sat with me on the Cape Elizabeth Youth Football board, took Jon from the bar to the men's restroom one floor down. He did this exactly once. Jon couldn't be trusted to navigate the terrain, though, surely, he knew where to go. In any case, this friend offered to take Jon to the men's room, and, since I am not a man, I accepted. I was happy to not be the person hanging around outside the men's room for a change. They were gone for what seemed like a long time. Apparently, there was some negotiation on how much time is appropriate for hand washing. I don't think this was the same night. Eventually, we moved "off-campus" from our slope-side condo to a house a few miles away.

Après dropped away with that move.

The lesson here might be that if you know that you want to do something then you need to make it happen. Barriers be damned.

So, one of the things about skiing at Sugarloaf is that you can often come across someone celebrating something. Anything, really.

This was the case one when Saturday afternoon when Jon and I took a quick bathroom and warm-up break at Bullwinkle's, the mid-Mountain restaurant and bar.

When I took him to the men's restroom, I always pointed to the water fountain between the men's and women's rooms and told him to wait for me there if he made it out first.

That never happened.

So, on this day, and after some time, where I assume, he was playing in the sink, Jon joined me by the water fountain. He then proceeded to go into the bar area. He was a very cute, and small, ten-year-old and could get away with such things as bar hopping.

It was at the bar that we came upon a bachelorette party. Lots of boas and a tiara. Just the kind of stuff that Jon loved.

I only met the bride to be once but knew some of the other attendees, so I stopped to chat for a bit.

Jon, always attracted to shiny things, took a liking to the bride-to-be and her tiara. Her pink feather boa was just a bonus for him.

She was very good with Jon and let him wrap himself up in the pink boa. They were getting along marvelously, and I actually thanked the bride-to-be for her kindness to my son.

It was after that when I noticed the strategically placed lifesavers sewn on her ski sweater. By the time I spotted them you can be sure that Jon had as well. And he went in for the kill, consuming many of those strategically placed candies.

There is photographic evidence of Jon biting these Lifesavers. I thought I might die. We said our hasty goodbyes, and everyone had a good laugh. This is a day that I won't forget.

When Jon was smaller, he was always climbing on the back of the furniture. Why he did this, I have no idea. There was one particular loveseat that wasn't up against a wall. It was at the ski house and there was a huge window and about eight feet away next to the dining table. This window became almost a mirror at night when the dark night outside contrasted with the low lights in the house. Bobby used the 'mirror' to check his surfing skills. Jon just surfed. Things were a little more relaxed at Sugarloaf. This furniture surfing seemed to be a favorite activity for Jon. He would walk back and forth and sense if the loveseat was about to tip. He hasn't actually tried surfing, but it's something I think he'd be very good at. He would move slightly to right the ship, err, loveseat before someone would tell him to get down. I didn't encourage this, but I did encounter it quite frequently. It was especially distressing at other's homes. My mom could never understand this behavior, though her own son (my brother) when he was young, wrote all over those pink velvety loveseats in permanent marker, that were recovered in a twill blue pattern and shipped to the ski house.

It's all a battle-just to what degree?

His great balance is probably why he would agree to walk parts of the Appalachian Trail with me. These small parts had areas where the trail was lined with planks that would keep hikers off the wet or muddy ground. Many hikers pay close attention to these boards, but Jon would just skip along happily, barely paying any attention to his navigation. We hiked in from Route 4 in Maine to Piazza rock. It's about two miles into this huge rock that you can shimmy through and climb to the top. He was having no part of the shimming thing and we didn't make it to the top, which I find interesting based on his earlier antics, but it's fun to watch him where he can be happy and safe!

We did several other hikes, including walking up Sugarloaf Mountain to the on-mountain restaurant one fall day. Several members of our party pooped out at fewer than 500 feet in elevation, but

Jon and I persevered. My goal was to have a beer on the empty deck. I have no idea what motivated Jon that day.

I wasn't always with Jon, but I was always with him when he had new staff. There were many times when I'd be breaking in a new in-home support person and Jon would go off and do something that looks dangerous. These people were sometimes alarmed by his 'agility' and would look concerned. I remember advising, more than once, to not get worried until I looked worried. This attitude of mine was often mistaken for being too laid back, but I truly knew what he was capable of, and when he might be in danger.

These are the subtleties of autism parenting.

This brings to mind times when I knew Jon was safe, but other people around him would look worried for his safety. Not caregivers, but people who shared the same space. I would often try to curtail his activity if people looked concerned, but not always. He did enjoy it, after all. He would often pace the bleachers at his brother's sporting events. In the beginning, the bleachers weren't too high so the risk wasn't as great. T-ball was played in a park by the ocean with concrete bleachers. This amphitheater was built into a hill with a wide area to sit or walk as was the case with Jon. He would go to the top one and just pace back and forth during the game. I would sit near the top to keep an eye on him, but not on the top step because that would spoil his fun. He liked to be alone up there!

Little League bleachers were too crowded for Jon to roam so he stopped for a couple of years. During the year of chemo, we just sat in my car with the radio on and watched from there. I watched. He happily monitored the radio.

Later, high school football bleachers came into play. The home bleachers were very high and made of splintering wood. They were scary for any fan. They had a rail across the back so the 15 or so foot drop wasn't too much of a worry, but a misstep could cause a forward tumble that would sting a bit. Freshman and JV football provided lots of time to bleacher walk, but Varsity was too crowded, and I usually tried to get a sitter to stay home with Jon. At least for home games. Away bleachers at any age were a crapshoot.

There was that one time when Bobby was playing on the road about 90 minutes away. I was getting ready for the long ride. Toys, snacks, blankets-all the essentials of Friday night lights in northern Maine in October. I turned my back and Jon scooped up his nighttime meds that I was preparing for the ride home-I think Dave was with the coaching staff that night. It was a very quiet game as his melatonin and Ambien kicked in just about when we got to the stadium and before the game even started. I was fully in charge of a drunk-looking Jon for that whole and long game. I have to admit that the parents that I thought were the most judgmental were the most understanding of this particular predicament.

Life is interesting.

The worst bleachers were the ones for high school, Babe Ruth, and American Legion baseball. They were the movable metal ones that had no side rails or backs. They weren't very high, but still, a tumble from the top would surely hurt. There were bleachers on both sides of the field, and both were always placed under a small tree. I only mention this because he would pace the top bleacher and grab a tree branch and defoliate it; tearing leaves off and watching as pieces floated to the ground. There was one fan-the parent of a teammate of Bobby's-who would get especially nervous if Jon was pacing behind him. Most people would comment on the strange behavior and go back to watching the game, but this man couldn't do that. I would do my best to get Jon down and otherwise occupied so that this man and I could both pay attention to the game and not the trickster who was multi-tasking pacing and tree destruction.

Speaking of trees, there was a great big white birch in my front yard in Cape Elizabeth when Jon was young. It was amazing for climbing, something white birches are not generally known for as they often grow straight and tall in Maine. This tree had a big, fat limb that came out at a perfect 90-degree angle and was about shoulder height for me. Perfect for perching small boys before they were big enough to climb up themselves. I have many pictures of the boys in that tree. One might even have been a Christmas card. I would sometimes lift Jon onto the branch if I was weeding the garden. He was happy to stand on it and watch the cars go by on the side road. I could get my work done and I knew that he was safe.

So safe, in fact, that when my carbon monoxide detector went off, and I had a headache that had me relegated to the couch, I called 911. I had no idea that four fire trucks and an ambulance would show up but show up they did and with sirens blaring. The firefighters checked the house and the EMTs checked me. The firefighters detected none of the deadly gas, but the EMTs suggested I take a hit of oxygen in the ambulance for some relief from that headache. I've suffered from headaches since I was young and this one stopped me in my tracks! I was worried about Jon running away so I suggested that the EMT assigned to watch Jon put him in the tree. Much easier and safer than trying to keep him from running or pulling some stunt. And, really, I wasn't in the mood to explain the situation. It was a strange suggestion, and I'm sure a first for that EMT, but Jon was put into the tree and was very happy and safe. The oxygen was amazing, and my headache dissipated. The suspected cause of the alarm was the combination of bleach in the basement from doing laundry mixing with bathroom cleaner on the second floor and meeting somewhere in the middle in the laundry chute that ran through the house.

The moral here is to not mix chemicals. That or clean less often.

One really hot summer in western Maine Bobby had a series of Babe Ruth baseball tournaments in a lake town about an hour away. Jon and I drove to watch these seemingly endless baseball games. Bobby rode early with his father who was helping coach. Jon and I showed up at game time and sat on the incredibly uncomfortable metal bleachers that soaked up the sun in the treeless 'Field of Dreams' in this tiny town. Those bleachers could, and did, burn any exposed skin, and all the water and Gatorade in the cooler couldn't keep us fully hydrated or cool.

In between games, when others were off getting food at local restaurants and taking a break from the heat, I would take Jon to the local lake. We picnicked in the shade and one day I allowed Jon to go into the lake. He decided to swim out to the float that was just offshore. I was about knee-high in the warm lake water when I let him go and watched his progress as he aimed for that float. He swam out in his strange jerking style and found the ladder to get on the float. There were several people getting on and jumping off the float at that time. I was surprised that he wanted to join the crowd but join he did. I could see him standing with the others. He was flapping his arms as he was wont to do. Soon, everyone jumped off the float and no one climbed back on. He had the float to himself. Perhaps that was the plan all along. I remember wondering how I was going to get him back to shore-short of swimming out and dragging him back. I was not wearing a swimsuit and had another baseball game to watch. Seven more innings in wet clothes did not appeal. The float was far enough away that Jon could pretend to not hear me call him back. He really seemed to be enjoying having that float to himself.

Eventually, he came back to me. Probably for a snack. In any case, he dried off and we headed back to the arid field for more baseball before heading home just to turn around and do the same thing the next day. Minus the lake swimming. I just wasn't up for that!

Many years later we took a family vacation to East Hampton in New York. East Hampton is on the ocean side and not the calmer Long Island sound side so the waves were incredibly fun to jump into and over. My brother, his wife, and dog joined us for the week. We rented a house with a pool, which only the dogs and Jon really used.

We had little use for the crowded beach during the day. Also, the parking was crazy! We would, however, take a to-go adult beverage to the beach around 5 PM, when the lifeguards were off for the day, dogs were allowed to run wild, and parking was free. The first day that we did this Jon was in his swimsuit and the expectation was set. We didn't know that there were big signs saying that swimming wasn't allowed after five until after we were already there. We assessed the situation and decided for the peace of everyone to let Jon wade out a bit. He was happy and safe in the ocean and no Great Whites were in sight. Jon was in high school by this time and his broad shoulders could have been those of a linebacker.

Shortly after he went into the water, I turned to see five adults looking and pointing at Jon. I was alarmed at first and looked to see what they were seeing. What they were seeing was a fifteen-year-old non-verbal young man with autism breaking the rules, but they didn't know that. They saw someone successfully playing in the ocean despite the warning sign. They shucked off their clothes, and clad in swimsuits, proceeded to join Jon in the surf. Of course, I took a picture of this to document his superior leadership skills. They tried to engage with him, but he just waved his arms and threw water on his head. He probably grunted as well. I couldn't really hear over the roar of the surf.

~ ❖ ~

At some point in high school, Jon discovered tie-dye. It became quite apparent that he was very attracted to all the colors and different patterns that the tie-dye presents. Because this seemed to please Jon, he accumulated quite a collection of tie-dye. To this day he still has a tie-dye blanket and beach towel as well as several T-shirts in various stages of disrepair as he often chooses to wear them over other, more subtle, T-shirts that might be in his drawer. He also has tie-dye curtains in his bedroom. He's hard to buy gifts for so I am unashamed that I often go back to that tie-dye well.

Jon has always walked with a certain confidence that seems incongruous with a person who is attended 24/7 and cannot speak. This confidence is evident wherever Jon is and with whatever he might be wearing. Tie-dye shirt with bright green shorts? No problem. It's just an expression of Jon's own hippie/preppy style.

Jon's full-grown adult height is only 5'7" and his inseam is 28 inches, so he doesn't appear to have the body of the male models that you see in catalogs. This never stopped Jon from wearing what he liked. And, sometimes what he liked were things that most of us would never put together. Woodstock meets Nantucket.

A few years ago, Jon had a favorite white polo shirt with thick horizontal navy stripes. This shirt looked great with jeans or chinos, but Jon decided one summer day that he would also wear this with his preppy plaid shorts, which hung low on his hips and hit at the knee. When he first put together this particular combination, complete with a popped collar, I was tempted to ask him to change. Who pulled off stripes and plaid? But Jon walked around with such confidence and acted so comfortable in his skin that I let it go. I thought it would be a one-time thing, but that outfit was in constant rotation that summer and subsequent summers until the shirt fell apart from the constant biting of the buttons, something he has always done when he gets frustrated.

It was after two summers of this outfit when I saw the cover model on a J. Crew catalog wearing a white polo with thick horizontal navy stripes, collar popped, and colorful and preppy plaid shorts that hit at the knee. I finally saw what Jon had known all along. You can wear what makes you feel good — and as long as you wear it with confidence, you will look good.

This is a lesson that I wished I'd learned long ago. I feel that most people are way too concerned and worried about putting pieces together. I learned from Jon that if you like it and it makes you happy then wear it and rock it.

I've established that Jon likes water. It's been an ongoing theme with him for, basically, ever. Lakes, pools, oceans, dog bowls-any water, anywhere.

I've also established that Jon liked to ski and that when he was young, we had a ski house.

This four-bedroom, two-bath house was located by Sugarloaf Mountain in western Maine. It was perfect because there was enough room for friends, (Bobby) and enough privacy for tantrums or a late-night giggle-fest depending on his mood, (Jon). It was acquired after a three-bed two bath condo on the mountain was too loud. The house came with more driving for the adults and less worrying about the kids getting woken up at night or waking others in a nearby condo. It was the definition of compromise.

One of the bathrooms had a whirlpool tub. Jon typically liked to shower as he got older, but this tub held a lot of appeal. It took a long time to fill, but once full, he could fully submerge, turn on the jets and soak away the aches from a day on the hill.

Jon especially liked it when I threw a bath balm or bubble bath into the running water. Lots of lovely smells and bubbles on those nights.

There was this one night in particular when Jon asked to use the tub. This was a normal Friday night routine for him even though he had no ski aches to soothe yet. I'm sure it was just a sensory thing.

Once I turned the taps on Jon disrobed in the bathroom and promptly threw his clothes out into the hall as he always did. I, in turn, left a towel, clean underwear (boxer briefs, only), and his PJ's on the stairs by the bathroom door. Somewhere along the way, and prior to this, he became bowel trained during the day and overnight!

He jumped right in regardless of the water level or temperature in the tub. I always came back to check on him and ask if he was ready for the jets that were controlled on the wall near the shower stall. He hardly ever started the jets by himself, but if he did, and the tub wasn't full, what a mess he could create. You really shouldn't turn the jets on until they are fully covered by water. For this reason, I didn't want Jon operating the controls.

Usually, I would let the tub fill for 15 minutes or so before going downstairs to check on Jon and to see if he was ready for the jets. He always was.

This one night that I'm thinking about started off fine. I filled the tub, added some bubble bath, and went upstairs to watch the news. During a commercial break, I checked in with Jon, turned off the water, and turned on the jets. I went back upstairs to continue watching the local news. Then, I lost track of time.

The bathroom door was directly at the bottom of the stairs from the living area to the bottom floor sleeping area. When I realized that the happy sounds of water play had noticeably diminished, I went to the top of the stairs. To my horror, I saw lots of bubbles oozing out from under the bathroom door-the door that I hadn't even closed. These bubbles were reminiscent of every '70's sitcom where some kid is doing laundry for the first time and puts too much soap in the machine. Way too much soap. Think The Brady Bunch.

Without Alice to help.

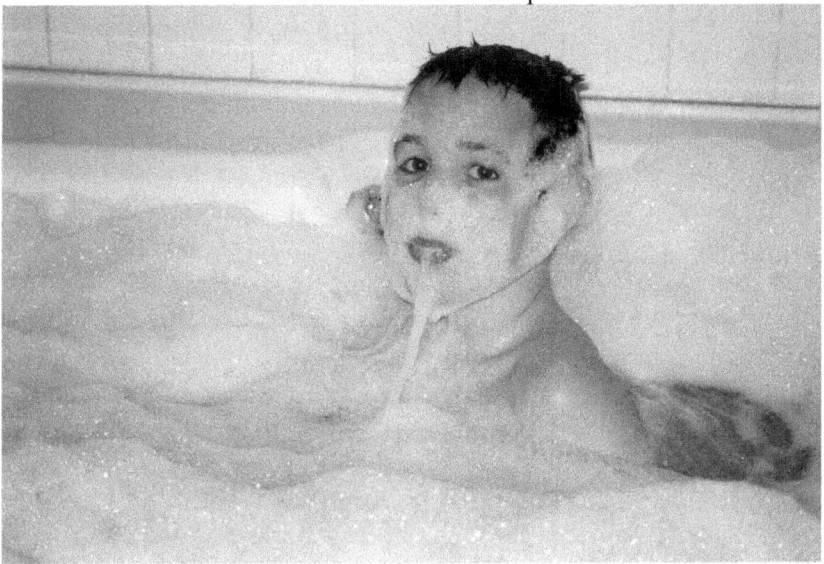

I ran down the stairs, and to my dismay, the bathroom door was locked. The bubbles continued to ooze under the door onto the green hall carpet that was either once fashionable or a really good deal, and in either case not particularly attractive. The water had been turned back on and I could hear the jets running.

A locked bathroom door wasn't a new thing and for that very reason, I kept one of those lock pickers hanging on the outside of the doors with interior locks. I quickly gained entry to the steamy, and very bubbly, room and stopped the jets and the water that Jon had turned back on.

That bathroom floor had never been so clean and I'm guessing it hasn't been that clean since. Lots of towels were sacrificed for the cause. Luckily, I had a washer and dryer for those towels-no soap needed.

Jon currently lives in an area where there are resources for children and adults with intellectual disabilities (ID).

Maine is a beautiful part of the world and Pine Tree Camp (PTC) is an idyllic spot in Maine, and only 30 minutes from Jon's house. Located directly on a lake, PTC is exclusively for people of all ages with disabilities, to enjoy five days at an overnight summer camp. Jon, and other campers at PTC, have a high need for care and supervision so a regular camp doesn't work well. Really, it doesn't work at all. Jon has attended PTC several times, but there is one time that sticks out in my mind.

While there is a trained counseling staff, they also have college students on hand to help, many of whom are interested in working with this population after graduation. The year that I'm remembering there were several support staff from a British-speaking part of the world; their accents were lovely.

We made our way through the registration and medical tents where each dose of his many meds had been bubbled packed for the safety of all campers. We met some of the staff. Specifically, we met some of the young British men with their charming accents. I happily filled them in on what they might need to know and left camp feeling that Jon would have a good week and a nice break from his normal routine.

Five short days later I returned to find Jon sitting at a long table with a bunch of happy campers as they ate lunch.

About two minutes after I approached Jon, I found myself surrounded by about five of those young British men. They were adorable and so excited to tell me all about Jon's camping experience, which basically started and ended with his time spent in the lake. OK, there may have been some talk about his love for ice cream, as well.

To my great relief, Jon did not jump off any boats. I don't think he even went on any boats that week. The big story was how he would stand waist-deep in the lake and, repeatedly, pour a bucket of water over his head. A trick he'd been doing for years in lakes, oceans, and bathtubs.

I acted very interested in this story because the tellers of this story were so enthusiastic and animated. I always love a happy Jon story.

It's not the first time that I've been told about some little strange thing that Jon does. In almost every case, I've seen the little strange thing before. He does love the feel of water on his head, as I've continued to mention. What I loved this day was the sheer enthusiasm from the counselors as they shared the story of Jon being Jon.

Another strange thing that Jon taught himself to do was to fling water from his hands into the air only to feel that same water run through those same fingers on the way back through. He would do this waist-high in the ocean and dip his head into the falling water before it hit his waiting hands. It was not uncommon to see smaller children trying to mimic this move. It's not as easy as it sounds, and few were as successful.

When Jon was a tween, he took this game just a bit farther. He would walk along the sand at the beach by the waterline, where it was still wet from the tide. He curled the toes on his right foot and kicked the wet sand up in the air behind him. This wet sand would land on his head like a soccer player heading the ball. He then tilted his head just so and caught the wet sand with his hands. He would do this without awareness of the audience that was so awed by this talent. He would just keep walking and tossing sand.

We could all learn from this. Be a little more 'Jon'.

As I've mentioned and is often the case with people with autism, Jon loves the water. I had no idea what I was in for when a family photo taken when he was 16 months old pictured him bending over with his head in the ocean. Same story with his head in the dog's water bowl, but this isn't about the strange places Jon chose to put his head. The is about boats: motorized and non-motorized. Because boats belong in the water.

One time I was kayaking with friends. Jon was in the kayak in front of me, a tandem, with his father. Jon was wearing a life jacket and watching the water from the 'back seat'. I was watching Jon.

Watching, I noticed a very peculiar thing that surprised me. He was really good about keeping his life jacket on-until he wasn't. After a few minutes in the kayak, I noticed him unzipping his life jacket. He then took the jacket off and quickly slithered into the lake and began to swim behind the kayak. Over the course of our outing, he did this several times so I'm certain it wasn't an accident.

He's a very capable swimmer so I let Jon swim behind his father's two-seater kayak. I kayaked behind Jon, and we stayed close to shore for safety. The water looked like it contained Milfoil, an invasive water plant. I was more worried about him swimming in the Milfoil than I was him swimming without a life jacket. When he was tired or when I thought it was time for him to get back into the kayak, his father pulled over to one of the many docks that lined the lake. Jon climbed out of the water and onto the dock and got back into the kayak. Thankfully no one objected to our using their private docks that day. He was very good about putting his life jacket back on. I have no idea if he understood the purpose of it, but, clearly, he knew that wearing it in the water would hamper his fun. By Maine law, Jon didn't have to wear the life jacket-it just had to be on the boat. Jon seems to like straddling the line of the law.

Another time I was at a different lake with Jon and his in-home support person. We were just hanging out. He was wading around by the sandy and rocky beach and the adults were watching and talking. A young man in a powerboat came over to strike up a conversation. He may have been about the same age as Jon's in-home support person, and, in retrospect, she was undoubtedly the attraction. It doesn't really matter. We got to talking and the young man with the boat offered us a ride. We were all very surprised when I agreed and said that Jon would like that very much. It was very hot and I thought it might be nice for everyone to cool off.

We headed out to the middle of the lake and the boat picked up speed. The wind in our faces felt fabulous. All of a sudden, you guessed it, Jon jumped out of the speeding boat. It wasn't so much of a jump as a slither off the side. Regardless, he was in the water and our new friend and host had to stop and turn the boat to retrieve the adventurous Jon. It was hard to contain Jon for the ride back to the dock. We never saw our new friend again.

I have pictures of him on commercial boats and ferries. There is always someone holding on to him to prevent his jumping off. That would be really bad-Jon jumping off a Casco Bay Ferry!

I can honestly say that I've jumped off party boats in the Caribbean, but that was way after Jon made his jumps and I'm pretty sure I haven't shared those stories with Jon.

Jon graduated from high school in 2011 at the age of 20. Getting senior photos taken in the fall of senior year is a tradition for most seniors and their families. What to wear? Where to have it taken? Do I dare include a pet? Bold move, by the way.

A tradition that I personally dreaded when it came to Jon. This was going to be a photoshoot with just Jon. No one to anchor him to stay in the frame. This photo would be in the yearbook and live on forever. This was a big deal.

The photographer that I chose was game to give this tradition a try with Jon. We chose a nearby field for the shoot. There would be no babbling brooks or waterfalls in the background. That would be just too risky! I had plenty of pictures of Jon in water-none of them appropriate for the yearbook. So, one September afternoon we headed off to the field. Jon was cleanly shaven with his hair combed down on his large head. I was accompanied by Jon's in-home support person, who was still providing in-home support as she worked on a master's degree in special education. We were armed with gummy bears, which of course were, to appropriately modify any deviant behavior.

The photographer let Jon roam around a bit and worked to make him comfortable. When she started shooting, he barely noticed. She shot for about 30 minutes. Jon only had one change of shirt-nothing too fancy, here. The shoot provided us with dozens of photos and many of them were shots that we could actually use! I have absolutely no idea which proof I chose for his yearbook shot after all that worry about the photo living in infamy, but I picked three 4x6 favorites and put them in a black wooden frame with a white mat that separated them from each other. I still display it in my home. Those three photos captured Jon so well.

At some point in his development, Jon started to cluck. He did this with his tongue, and it was usually a happy thing. He would cluck and I would cluck back then he would cluck again. It was a thing that he did with people he trusted. I'm not sure which of us was clucking with Jon when the photographer got the perfect shot. Jon, wearing a black polo shirt with the collar popped was caught in mid-cluck. He had his mouth wide open. His adult teeth were not as pearly and perfect as his baby ones were, but they are still strong and white, and somehow, he never needed braces. He was also graced without wisdom teeth so those were two dodged bullets in my book! Anyway, his tongue was perfectly positioned for a cluck-the tip touched the roof of his mouth and was hidden behind his teeth. The green background was a stand of trees that were blurred to showcase Jon's beautiful and happy face.

The middle picture is in black and white, and Jon was still wearing the black polo with the collar still popped. Jon was looking straight at the camera and his dark hair was cut short. It was already starting to recede. His amber eyes looked dark in the black and white format and his dark brows perfectly covered the space just over his eyes. Jon had both hands covering his mouth. This is something that he sometimes did when he didn't want to hear something. He's not angry or defiant. He just covered his mouth with his large hands while his adult-sized forearms sat across his broad chest.

The final picture of my trio had Jon wearing a navy and white striped polo with a huge blue horse on the chest. Chaps brand with the navy-blue collar popped and shirt untucked, as usual. This look was all Jon. I had long ago lost any influence over his clothing choices or how he chose to wear his clothes. In this photo, Jon's eyes and mouth are wide open. He was probably looking at me because he had his left hand in the air, palm faced out, and waving goodbye. I could tell by his body language that he had already started to walk off. He still waves goodbye to me when he sees me. Something that I've had to accept over the years. This had to have been the last photo of the shoot. The light in the background was bright on the yellow foliage that lined the field in late September and shone on the left side of his face. If I had to guess, the next picture in the roll would be of the back of his head as he walked away.

His work was done and he did great with no one holding him in the frame!

Back in 2001, a disheveled man boarded a flight to the US with the intent of detonating a bomb that was hidden in his shoes. Luckily, his attempt failed, but flying in the US has been forever changed.

Removing shoes before going through security was never a problem for Jon. He has always loved to take his shoes off. In fact, he has always been the kid who didn't have shoes on when it was time to go somewhere.

Right before Jon graduated from high school, Dave and I took him to Florida for spring break. It wasn't the same trip as his brother, who brought a friend to the Dominican Republic, and being 18, smoke copious amounts of cigars in their hotel room. Disgusting. For Jon, it was a trip to Sanibel Island in Florida, where stingrays roamed the shores, the water was warm, and shells were abundant. No passport was needed!

Jon didn't really care about any of this.

Jon did like the condo and especially the hot tub and pool at the resort. But they were often crowded, and he's never really liked people. This nudged him towards the ocean. The west coast of Florida is nice and calm, and Jon prefers waves, but water is water.

He somehow made it past the stingrays that could be seen playing in the wave line. Travel guides advise people to wear water shoes and shuffle when moving past these sea creatures because they can flip their long tails around and sting unsuspecting people walking out to deeper waters. I don't think that Jon was ever stung as he always made it out to those deeper waters. Jon waded pretty far out and was still only up to his waist in the warm salty water as I watched from the water's edge. He never wore water shoes. Luckily, he is a solid swimmer and I never had to go rescue him because I was not as comfortable with those pesky stingrays. Shuffle or no shuffle. Water shoes or not.

After dinner, we walked the beach to watch the sunset and I looked for interesting shells, while the sun put on a beautiful show as it set over the horizon. We saw people fishing up at the point and even saw someone reel in a small shark. Another reason that I was glad to stay ashore, but I was now worried about two kinds of sea-beasts and Jon in those deeper, but still not deep waters!

After five days of Florida sunshine, Jon was browned up like a berry, as a friend's mom used to say. His olive-colored skin was a good match for the April sun, which is excellent because he's always been a bit averse to wearing sunscreen. I'll thank the Portuguese heritage on my mom's side for this and not the Irish/English mix that is not so friendly with the sun, that graces most of the rest of us.

At 20 years old, (students with intellectual disabilities can stay in public high school until the year that they turn 20), Jon was quite capable of growing a beard. I can't remember if it was an oversight on my part, but we didn't have a razor with us on that trip. He didn't particularly like to be shaved so perhaps I figured I'd give him a week off. His beard grows in very quickly, thick and dark. With his dark skin, amber eyes, and disheveled/unshaven face, well I'm not going to say that he looked like a terrorist, but his grunting didn't help his case.

So, back to the shoes. After a week of walking barefoot in Florida, it was time to return to the, still cold, Northeast. Shoes were a necessary part of this plan. Getting on the plane was not an issue. I remember hoping the people around us could tell that he was a disabled young man returning from vacation and not some loud, angry person who might want to harm them. When Jon wants something, he can be very loud, and if his grunts sound angry-they often are angry if he isn't getting his needs met. Planes are small and he is big, so this was a bit uncomfortable. It was also the last time that he flew.

Jon always had a thing about bathrooms. It seems that he never outgrew the curiosity that new bathrooms must be inspected and used in every possible place, and planes are no exception. He had this thing about taking off his shoes before entering a stall. I've never encouraged this; in fact, I've discouraged it. Often. There was a time when he would disrobe entirely, so just the shoes off seemed manageable and a welcomed change but could still be a pain in the neck. Think Seinfeld and George at the party with the bathroom disrobe. The only time Jon didn't take his shoes off was when he was skiing and wearing ski boots. He never could get his own boots on or off so that worked in the ski lodge, but we were on the plane, not the slopes.

Jon grunted enough to convince me that he really did need to visit the bathroom at the back of the plane-something that I was desperately hoping to avoid. I walked back with him and was bummed to see two flight attendants by the restroom. I caught a quick glimpse of their faces when Jon slipped out of his sneakers, walked into the restroom, and forcefully locked the door. I've had many occasions when I felt compelled to explain what's going on to people. I probably shouldn't, but I sometimes still do. I quickly explained that Jon has autism and would be perfectly safe in the bathroom. I also explained that I would stay right with him and guard his Reeboks until he was finished. It's funny now, I promise.

Eventually, Jon came out of the restroom and put his shoes back on. We returned to our seats and the rest of the flight was uneventful. It was a very nice pre-graduation vacation, and we did make memories. It just seems that the shoes on the plane is more vivid in my mind than the glorious sunsets we witnessed.

PART 4
AFTER THE MOVE

Raising Jon was hard. He changed many things about me. I realized that I no longer had as much control as I once thought when I had a very strong type-A personality. I truly feel that I would have continued with that if not for Jon. It's not a bad thing. Now, I no longer consider myself type-A. I know that I can't control everything. Jon taught me that.

A lot of these stories are about a younger Jon. A Jon who was learning his way through a world where most people communicate verbally. This is most often how our needs are met. This is a world where Jon had to learn a different way to get his needs met, after all. He seems to have succeeded at this. Most of the time.

Jon has lived independently from me for ten years now. It was a huge transition for me. Much harder than when Bobby went off to college: I had been working on that transition for years. Jon's transition was uncertain, for me, at least. Mostly due to funding. Jon had been on the state housing waitlist since he turned 18.

It was in May of 2012 when I learned that Jon had secured the necessary funding to live independently, but very supported, in a group home nearby. This was after a very emotional year of talking to legislators and anyone else who would listen to my story. I felt strongly that Jon needed to live independently from me. We had been velcroed together for so many years, but he was 21 years old and ready to be away from mom. It was a year with many challenges, including my relatively new job with a school system as a school counselor. I don't know exactly how Jon was deemed worthy in a system with, literally, hundreds of people waiting for funding, but he was, and the woman who called to tell me said, "It's like Christmas." We both cried.

In any case, after funding was secured, there was a process to get matched up with various agencies and services for day programs and 24/7 care. Jon's case manager sent out a vendor call, which was designed pretty specifically, to capture the interest of programs located within a ten-mile radius of my house. This very intentional plan worked very well for us.

Jon had an August 1 move-in date in a two-person home in the next town over. Day programs, being easier to coordinate, were already in place. I had had conversations with Jon, albeit one-way conversations, about his upcoming move. I had no idea if he understood what was happening. Dave's entire family was visiting, and we had a busy house that week. I'm sure they didn't see the best of me that day/week! It was hard work and very emotional.

On August 1, 2012, Jon left for his day program around nine am. At shortly after nine, the maintenance people from his new group home came to my house to get his furniture. They moved a bed, dresser, loveseat, and some smaller things along with all his clothes and sports gear. Furniture that had been replaced from his earlier rejection of a typical bedroom years earlier.

The loveseat had been in our family room. It was where Jon always sat. If you sat on it, he would make you feel very uncomfortable by pacing in front of you. Eventually, you would vacate his space and he could happily reclaim his seat. Regardless if other seats were open in the room and to be clear, there were lots of seats to choose from.

Occasionally, our 150 plus pound Newfoundland would perch herself up there. I believe that Wrigley knew that it was Jon's seat, but she had a sense of adventure, and Jon and Wrigley had a sibling relationship that included a strong rivalry. Jon needed only to touch her collar and she would get out of his territory and off the loveseat. She made everyone else in the family work harder to get her to move that majestic body.

The loveseat was transported, but not easily as it was very large, from our house to Jon's new living room. At 1:30, I picked Jon up from his day program and drove him to his new home. I was eager to see how well he made the connection between his loveseat and his new home. I had spent most of the day at his new place unpacking clothes, dishes, and sports equipment. I made his bed and moved the loveseat to where I thought he would be comfortable and most likely to make the connection as well as putting it in a straight line to the TV.

I walked into his new place with him at 2 PM and eagerly watched to see his reaction to his beloved, and well worn, brown leather loveseat and hopefully a connection that let me know he understood the significance of his furniture and his new home. He walked in the door, looked around, and immediately plopped his body down on a futon that neither of us had seen before that day. My grand plan did not work, for me at least, but Jon settled in very quickly.

Now, ten years later, I feel very comfortable that Jon understands his new 'independent from me' life. I know this because sometimes I would, pre-pandemic, pop into his current house, which was about a three-minute walk from my house before I recently moved, and he would always greet me with his semi-audible version of the word 'bye', pronounced 'buh' and an emphatic wave.

My cue to vacate his space.

At first, I took this personally, but now I take it as a sign that he is where he needs to be. And best of all, he is happy there!

My plan for this memoir of my time raising Jon was to end it when Jon moved out of my house in 2012. As I've been writing and remembering I have a couple of stories that happened after Jon moved out and show how he presents to the world as an adult.

He is still non-verbal and can be seen as the strong silent type. He does still exhibit behaviors that are truly hard to watch. He has taken to hitting himself on the forehead with a closed fist when he gets frustrated or upset. When he was younger, he would just grab his shirt and bite on it. He always wore true Rugby style shirts in the winter because of the rubber buttons that would protect his teeth. In warmer weather, he would bite his tee-shirt. This created a bunch of tiny holes that looked like pinpricks but were caused by those same teeth. Ruining clothes was frustrating, and he always had a revolving stack of shirts in various stages of disrepair. It was nothing compared to watching him hit his head. He now has a callous on his hand from striking his head right above and between his eyes. He also has a callous on his head from this as well. If he's had a bad few days that callous on his head can be quite red. He looks like he is turning into a unicorn. An angry unicorn if that's a thing. If he's had a bad few days, the callous on his hand will split open and bleed.

He has undergone so many diagnostic tests to figure out if there is an underlying cause. It appears to just be callous on callous. He even had a semi sedated MRI to look for brain damage as I was convinced that he was continually concussing himself. Because he also has seizure disorder, we tried to get an EEG. I say we, but I didn't go. He went with two very patient Direct Support Professionals (DSPs) from his house. I had tried it once when he was younger. He rejected it outright and I was back on the road within an hour. This time, he freaked out and began hitting and screaming. I think he scared his doctor, which might have helped him in the long run because I don't think she ever thought his behavior could be that violent.

But this epilogue isn't about his seizures, struggles, or behavior. It's about how he can present himself in the world-especially when he is outside his safe home space.

~ ❖ ~

At some point in Jon's mid-twenties when Dave and I were still married. We rented a house in Kennebunkport as we used to when Jon was a young child. My mom came from Topsham to join us for the week at the beach and we brought Jon down for two nights. The first night was very uneventful. He didn't like the dog. Camden (again, a Newfoundland) wasn't his precious Wrigley, but he dealt with it with no issues or behaviors. He'd seen Cam before at our house and most likely had seen Cam as he was recovering from one of his six surgeries on his four legs. They seemed to have a pact to ignore each other.

We rented a three-bedroom house with a deck off the living room and a fenced yard. The beach wasn't within walking distance, but the ice cream shop was. The first night we went into town for dinner even though we had plenty of food to cook for ourselves. We went early to a pub-style restaurant, which seemed like the best bet for Jon. We were served pretty quickly and there were no problems that I recall. Back to the house. Out for ice cream. Back to the house and a movie before bed. The next day was warm and sunny and Dave and I took Jon to the beach while my mom read on the deck. We had two chairs, but Jon doesn't usually sit long in a beach chair, so we didn't worry much about one for him. He was wearing his neon green swim shorts that he loved and could pull off with his darker coloring. The sand and the water were both a bit crowded, but Jon still decided to go swimming for a bit. We took turns keeping an eye on him while the other read or napped. He was in the water for about a half-hour doing his Jaws routine of dunking and bobbing and squealing before he came back looking for the lunch that we had packed.

After lunch, we walked to the end of the beach that is typically less crowded. That end had private parking only so only the people in those houses could access that prime real estate which really kept the numbers down. We walked by families digging in the sand and building castles. We walked by young adults who were playing Can Jam or other beach games. We walked by sunbathers and people sitting under umbrellas, reading in the shade. It was a good walk even though Jon preferred to walk about five feet behind us. I didn't really blame him. What 20-something wants to be seen on the beach with mom and dad? I also noticed that several girls about his age were checking him out. He looked like he was walking alone. Broad shoulders nice and tan, strong legs also tan and looking more so against the bright green suit that was still wet and clung just so. His forehead was smooth and unmarred as this was years before the self-hitting began.

It was a surreal moment for me to see Jon as others might see him. As a normal and attractive young man. As a potential swipe right in the Tinder world.

I had been seeing him as others might see him for years, but that was through the lens of other grocery shoppers seeing a boy having a tantrum. I often wondered if these people thought he was just a brat or if they could tell that he had special needs. Once, when Jon was five and in the grocery store, in line, in fact. With a full cart. He started to meltdown. We'd been in the store for too long, but I had everything I needed. I just needed to get through the checkout. I can't remember what the problem was if I even knew, but I started making up signs. We weren't practicing ASL yet and I didn't know sign, but I felt like that would let people know that I was dealing with something a bit more than just a bratty or tired child who was clearly older than the terrible twos would allow for such behavior. I don't know why I cared, but it was one of the hardest parts of raising Jon-always feeling like I had to explain. Later when he was much older and bigger and apt to hit himself in the head I would notice that people near me in these grocery store lines moved away with looks of horror on their faces. By this time, I was way past caring and was pretty sure that he wasn't going to attack anyone. If I had an Ativan in my pocket, I gave it to Jon to settle him quickly. Often, the front-end manager of our local store saw us coming and opened a line for us.

Grace.

~ ❖ ~

That night, after the beach, we ate on the deck while the dog roamed around the yard-giving Jon lots of space. Again, we watched a movie after Jon showered and got ready for bed. He was restless. He watched for a bit and then went into his room. The small room with bunk beds. He went into his duffle bag and pulled out an outfit and changed into it. He did this at least three times. He came into the living room dressed in shorts and a tee and then different shorts and a polo and one more time in another outfit. He was packed for a week for his two-day stay. Jon has a tendency to get messy and his group home sent preparation for all situations. It wasn't until much later that I figured out that perhaps all this changing was his way of trying to communicate that he wanted to go home. Which outfit was the right one to wear for the two-hour ride back to his group home? While we were watching him do this, we thought it was kind of cute.

If I'm correct in my supposition and being perfectly honest, it's kind of heartbreaking.

He had a rough night that night-not sleeping well. The next morning, we took him to walk the beach with the dog. He was too tired to protest. I have a picture of him following my Newfoundland, Camden in the morning fog. Other people were in the distant background and Jon looked off to the side. He was wearing a white polo shirt with navy stripes and Kelly-green shorts. His face was serious but calm. The polo shirt clung to his broad shoulders and was loose on his slim torso. He could be in a magazine shoot. It's a picture that I have framed.

He slept all the way home in the car that day. I can probably count on one hand the number of times that he actually fell asleep in the car in his life. Even on those long rides to Virginia, he was mostly wide awake. That visit was a roller coaster of emotions for all of us and I think it took the rest of the week to recover.

~ ❖ ~

Jon has four housemates now and has moved to a bigger house in town. These young people have a variety of abilities and interests. It's an interesting house and there is always something going on. The group home is just one of many in a larger organization. This allows even more people with abilities and interests to congregate and celebrate life or holidays or whatever happens when people get together. At one point, Jon's house walked into town and joined the college kids at an open mic night at a local bar. I always said that I would make it down to see them at open mic. A couple of his housemates played the guitar and I'd seen them practice at the house. I never did make it to one of those nights and they all stopped going when there was a fight that had nothing to do with them but spoiled the fun for the house.

One night after dinner when I was still married, Dave and I walked down to a different local bar. We sat at the bar and talked with the bartender as we sometimes did back them. There was another couple sitting next to us doing the same thing. Eventually, we started chatting with them a bit.

We were talking about Jon and our want to see him at open mic night sometime. This was before the fight. To be clear- we never thought that he would get up and play or sing any music. It was just our wanting to see him in an age-appropriate activity while drinking Ginger Ale.

I was describing one of Jon's housemates and how he played the guitar and the couple next to us got really excited. They were sure that they knew the young man I was talking about. They told us his name. Bingo. At first, it was just one of those coincidences and we laughed. They asked about Jon and we told them that he was non-verbal with autism and wasn't likely to be on stage. They got a little more excited because they had been to open mic night to support Jon's housemate.

"Is he the guy that paces around? He has dark hair and a goatee and doesn't talk to anyone. He just walks around watching people and occasionally flaps his arms around." Yup. We had never witnessed this, but it sure sounded like our guy.

"We thought that he was staff until he started flapping his hands. Then he went to a table with a couple of women and got ice cream."

Was that a 'proud mom' moment? A 'what could have been' moment? A, 'wow, they nailed it', moment?

Jon has a long-term (at least five years) goal to stay on task for two hours with only verbal prompts. This goal is so that he can be reevaluated by Voc Rehab to see if he might have the skills (and more importantly, attention span) to someday hold a part-time job. To think that these people thought, even for a moment, that he was in a position of responsibility, given that he is under 24/7 care, was a little mind-blowing for me. And, again, a lot heartbreaking.

When I'm with Jon I'm always looking for the possible pitfalls: dogs that might jump or bark, babies who might cry, motorcyclists who might rev their engines-especially when he covers his ears (asshole behavior), and any other thing that might cause him distress. In fact, I've been doing this for so long that I notice all these things even when he's not around. It's like I can't turn it off. A constant reminder that I have responsibilities beyond my day-to-day life.

A greater purpose.

A reason to write a memoir.

www.ingramcontent.com/pod-product-compliance
Lightning Source LLC
LaVergne TN
LVHW051838080426
835512LV00018B/2948